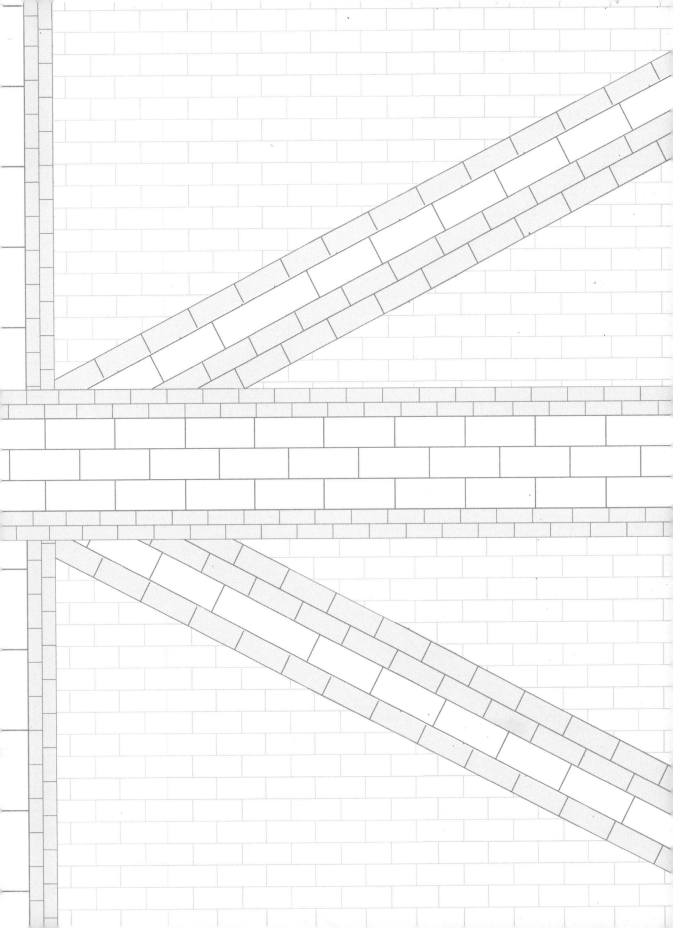

THE HAIRY BIKERS'
BRITISH CLASSICS

Si King & Dave Myers

THE HAIRY BIKERS'
BRITISH
CLASSICS

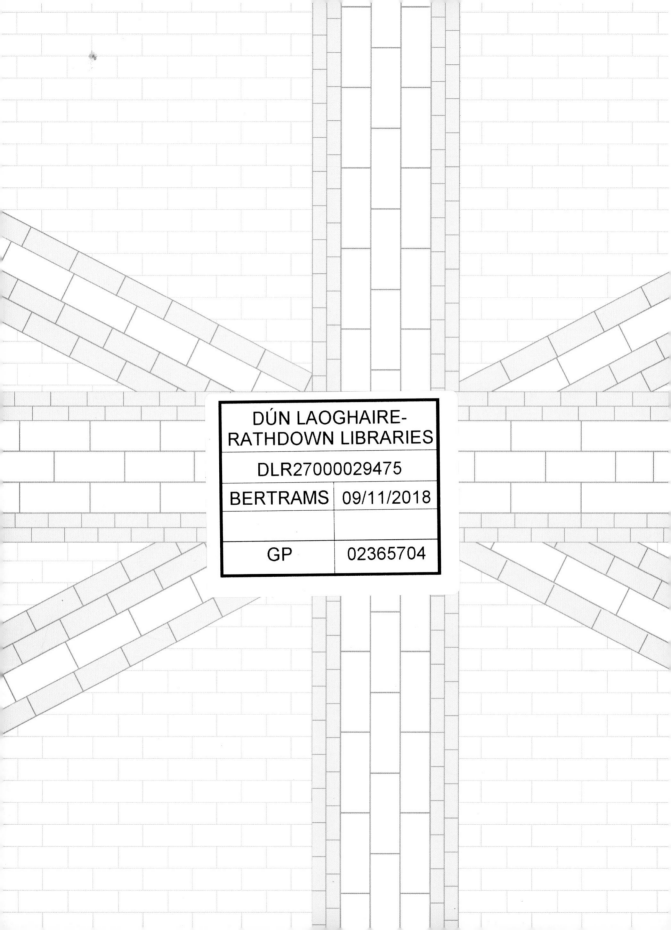

CONTENTS

Welcome to our British classics

Hello everyone and welcome to our great new collection of favourite recipes.

We've both been cooking since we were children, but our adventures with food really took off when we first met in 1992 while working on the set of a Catherine Cookson drama called *The Gambling Man*. And we haven't looked back. We chucked our day jobs and we've been cooking and writing and filming about food ever since.

We've had a lifelong love affair with food and we want to share that with you, bringing you some of the classic dishes that we've cooked over the years – and some new ones too. We've been involved in the production of more than 2,000 recipes and from those we've selected our favourites – and by heck it's been a job to whittle them down. These are our go-to recipes, the ones we make over and over again at home for our friends and family. Some you'll know from our telly programmes, others are new versions of old favourites. Most haven't been published before but there are a few that we just love so much we had to include them here. It's an eclectic mix but each dish is a bit of a stunner and has really earned its place in our hearts and in our stomachs.

Since we started our cooking lives, the idea of what makes a British classic has changed hugely. Yes, we still love steak and kidney pud, roast chicken, toad in the hole and apple pie, but we've embraced the food of other countries too, and we've made some of their classics our own. Chicken tikka masala was voted Britain's favourite dish a few years ago, and there's a tandoori house on every high street. Thai curries feature in supermarket ready-meal ranges, and pulled pork and Caribbean jerk chicken have made their way on to our barbecues. We all have packets of pasta in our cupboards, and lasagne and pizza are some of our best-loved foods.

That's why in this book you'll find curries, pasta and paella alongside roast pork and apple crumble. There's quiche Lorraine as well as cheese and onion pie, and cheesecake and pavlova as well as Madeira cake and jam roly poly. Our choice of classics reflects the way we eat today and the reality of our multicultural land. We Brits have a great ability to cherry-pick the best of the cuisines of other countries. It's what keeps our cooking alive, fresh and inventive – and why we never get bored in the kitchen. Both at home and on our travels, we've met so many great people who've inspired us, shared their cooking secrets and introduced us to dishes that have become part of our lives.

Our aim with this book is to bring you some of our favourite classic recipes and make them satisfying and achievable. This is NOT a diet book and not a collection based on food fads and cutting-edge cheffy techniques. It's a book of familiar food to bring joy and comfort in this increasingly hectic world. We want to make cooking, fun so time in the kitchen is not a chore but a chance to enjoy making food for those you love. Food is love, after all, and without love it's just a plate of stuff.

Dave:

I was born greedy. When I was a lad, food was the centre of our family life – as it was in most northern households. I was never allowed to go off to school without an egg for breakfast, and my mam cooked all our food every day. Monday was baking day and she would make Victoria sponge, white baps – all really good.

Even now, the thought of Sunday lunch brings back memories of the delicious smells of the roast in the oven, the sound of the pressure cooker hissing, the sight of bread rising under a tea towel in the kitchen fireplace.

But when I was only eight years old, Mam was diagnosed with multiple sclerosis, and by the time I was 12 I'd taken over all the shopping and cooking for the family. The first thing I ever cooked was a cheese and potato pie so my dad had something to eat when he got home from work. I soon learned to enjoy cooking and making what I wanted to eat. I would prepare beautiful salads to tempt my mam when she was feeling ill. I'd take great care to cut everything nicely, then ruin it all with a great dollop of salad cream.

I even made a bit of money from cooking. I made curries with eggs and sausages, then invited my mates round to my house to eat – cheaper than the local takeaway.

When I first went to uni in London I was blown away by the food that was on offer. In my first week I went for a curry – I knew about curry because we had curry powder in the larder at home. I ordered a chicken madras and some things I thought were giant crisps (poppadoms) and loved it all so much I vowed to eat my way through the menu. That ate through my grant pretty quickly too!

Throughout my student days I spent more time cooking and eating than studying art and I subjected my flatmates to my triumphs. I started to buy cookbooks. My culinary adventure had really taken off. And then I met Si.

Si:

I was born into a family of foodies. Mam was a fantastic cook and so were my dad, my brother and my sister. There were four topics of conversation in our house: football, politics, music and food. At every meal, we'd be talking about what to make for the next one.

My dad was in the Navy and would come home from his travels with exotic ingredients, such as unusual spices and lemongrass – I guess that's where my passion for spicy food comes from. Mam was never fazed by anything – she was a very creative, adventurous and instinctive cook. She did have lots of handwritten recipes handed down by family members but most of her dishes were in her head. I don't ever remember her making anything that wasn't delicious.

My dad died when I was quite young, and I started to cook a lot with my mam because we needed to spend time together after Dad's death. I learned to bake, roast, braise and fillet. I learned to celebrate food and what it meant – cooking for the people you love. In our house food was always an expression of love and care.

We always talked and laughed over our meals. And we always made too much. For generations, our family had cooked for miners, making big portions for hard-working men, and we still cooked plenty in case anyone else turned up for a meal. We couldn't bear the thought that anyone might go hungry – not much chance of that in our house!

It wasn't until I met Dave that I could have a proper conversation about food with someone outside the family. It was so great to find a mate who was just as enthusiastic about cooking and eating as me but had a different way of looking at things. For instance, Dave loves to mess around with a sous vide water bath thingy – doesn't appeal to me – but he couldn't be arsed to dig a fire pit, which is much more my style. When we cook together, I do the butchery, he does the fish filleting. When we're making a pie, Dave does the pastry and I make the filling.

We're a great team and it works.

Cooking for one or two

There are more than nine million two-person households in the UK, and more than seven million with only one person, so it's no wonder that we're often asked about how to scale down recipes, many of which are written for four. And in our own households the kids have moved out so we're often cooking for one or two – and then the next minute everyone's home for a family feast!

First off, for many recipes such as soups, stews and pasta, it's very easy to halve or quarter the ingredients. Just remember when adding seasoning and spice that it's easier to add more than take it out, so go easy at first and keep tasting. Cooking time won't necessarily be half the time given in the recipe so again, use your judgement and check carefully.

Another option is to make the full quantity, then portion it up and stash what you don't need immediately in the freezer for another day. Soups freeze really well, as do stews, meatballs, meatloaf and nut roast. Cakes, such as Madeira, you can cut in half or quarter and freeze for another day. Make a big batch of tomato sauce that you can freeze and then use with pasta or to serve with meatballs. Cook up some pulses or grains such as lentils and quinoa and freeze them in small portions to defrost when needed – saves so much time and effort.

A few little notes from us

Peel onions, garlic and other veg and fruit unless otherwise specified.

Use free-range eggs whenever possible. And we generally use large eggs in our recipes unless otherwise specified.

Weigh all your ingredients and use proper measuring spoons. We've made oven temperatures as accurate as possible, but all ovens are different so keep an eye on your dish and be prepared to cook it for a longer or shorter time if necessary.

A meat thermometer is a useful bit of kit if you want to be sure of perfectly cooked meat and poultry. You can buy one online for a reasonable price.

We've included a few stock recipes at the back of the book and they're great to have in your freezer. But if you don't have time, there are good fresh stocks available in the supermarkets or you can use the little stock pots or cubes.

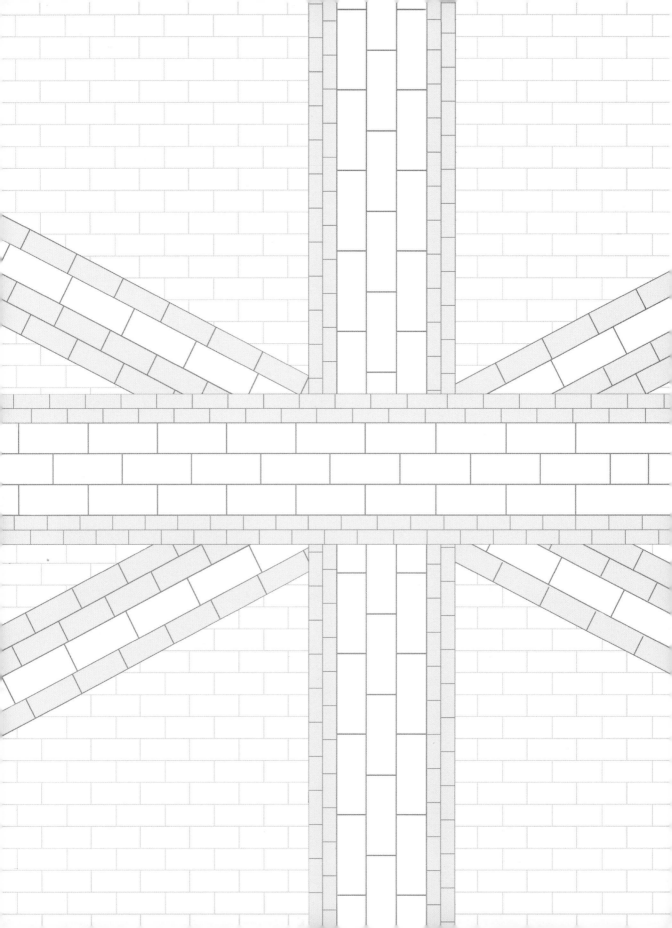

SUPER STARTERS, SOUPS AND SALADS

Red lentil and bacon soup 18

Parsnip and apple soup 20

Summer vegetable soup 22

Winter vegetable soup 24

Waldorf salad 26

Roast squash salad 28

Caesar salad 30

Prawn cocktail 32

Goats' cheese and chive soufflés 34

Devilled whitebait with green sauce 36

Squid with chilli and garlic dipping sauce 38

Pork and pistachio pâté 40

Pork and chicken terrine 42

Mini toad in the holes 44

Red lentil and bacon soup

This tasty, filling soup was inspired by the great ham hock and split pea soup that Si's mam used to make. That did take quite a while to cook but this recipe can be on the table in about 20 minutes. It's a firm favourite with us both and really comforting – central heating in a bowl we call it. It freezes really well too so if you like, you could portion it up and stash it in the freezer for those days when you're extra short of time.

Serves 6

1 tsp vegetable oil

75g smoked back bacon, finely chopped

1 onion, finely chopped

1 red pepper, finely chopped

1 small sweet potato, finely diced

1 garlic clove, chopped

200g red lentils, rinsed

1.5 litres hot chicken or vegetable stock

large thyme sprig

1 bay leaf

sea salt and black pepper

Heat the oil in a large pan and add the bacon, onion and red pepper. Cook over a low heat for 5 minutes, or until the vegetables have started to soften. Add the sweet potato, garlic and lentils and stir for a minute or so.

Pour the hot stock into the pan, add the herbs and season with salt and pepper. Turn up the heat and bring the soup to the boil, then turn the heat down to medium and cover the pan. Cook for 15–20 minutes, or until the red lentils are tender.

Remove the herbs and serve. If you want a smooth soup, blitz it in a food processor or with a stick blender.

Parsnip and apple soup

We first tasted parsnip and apple soup at Leslie Castle in Aberdeenshire when we were filming there some years back and we've loved it ever since. The sweet parsnips and sharp apple go together perfectly. We like this soup with a hit of curry spice – if you fancy this idea, add a tablespoon of good old-fashioned Madras curry powder to the onions, parsnips and apple before pouring in the stock.

Serves 6

_____

25g butter

1 tbsp vegetable oil

2 medium onions, chopped

600g parsnips, cut into 2cm pieces

2 garlic cloves, crushed

600g Bramley apples, peeled, quartered and cut into chunks

1 litre hot vegetable or chicken stock

150ml milk

sea salt and black pepper

Melt the butter and oil in a large saucepan. Gently fry the onions and parsnips for about 15 minutes, or until the onions have softened. Add the garlic and apples, then cook for another couple of minutes, stirring regularly.

Pour over the stock and bring to the boil. Reduce the heat to a simmer and cook for about 20 minutes, or until the parsnips are very soft. Remove the pan from the heat and season the soup with salt and freshly ground black pepper. Blitz the mixture until smooth in a food processor or in the pan using a stick blender.

Stir in the milk, adding a little extra if required. Warm the soup through to serve and season to taste with salt and pepper.

Summer vegetable soup

Soup's not just for cold winter nights. We both love our veggies and in summer, when the most wonderful fresh produce is available in this country, we like to make beautiful seasonal soups like this one. It gives a good boost to your five a day – and fills you up with chlorophyll! The drizzle of home-made basil oil adds a nice touch of sunshine flavour. All you need is a nice hunk of bread to dunk and you'll be as happy as a Hairy Biker. *Si*: Dave loves to grow his own and even has a polytunnel!

Serves 6

―――――

1 tbsp olive oil

1 onion, finely chopped

1 celery stick, finely sliced

2 garlic cloves, finely sliced

1 young leek, trimmed
  and finely sliced

3 small courgettes,
  cut into 1cm dice

4 large ripe vine
  tomatoes, skinned

1.5 litres chicken stock

50g spaghetti

1 tbsp tomato purée

200g podded fresh or
  frozen peas

200g podded fresh or
  frozen baby broad beans

200g green beans,
  cut into short pieces

40g Parmesan cheese,
  grated

sea salt and black pepper

Basil oil

50g fresh basil

100ml olive oil

First make the basil oil. Strip the basil leaves from the stalks and put them in a large heatproof bowl. Fill another bowl with cold water and add a few ice cubes. Pour boiling water over the basil leaves, then immediately drain them in a colander and plunge them into the iced water. This will help set the vibrant green colour. Leave the basil for 5 minutes, then drain it again and pat it dry with kitchen paper. Put the leaves into a small food processor, add the oil and blend to a purée. Season with salt and pepper, then set aside for at least 30 minutes.

For the soup, heat the oil in a large pan and fry the onion and celery very gently for 5 minutes, stirring often. Don't allow them to colour. Add the garlic, leek and courgettes and stir over a low heat for a minute or so, then dice the tomatoes and add them to the pan. Pour over the chicken stock and bring to the boil.

Break the spaghetti into short pieces and drop them into the soup, then add the tomato purée and bring back to the boil. Cook for about 8 minutes, stirring occasionally. Add the peas, broad beans and green beans and cook for another 5 minutes, or until the pasta is just tender. Season with salt and plenty of black pepper.

Serve the soup in bowls with a drizzle of basil oil and sprinkle with Parmesan. Any leftover basil oil can be covered and kept in the fridge for up to 3 days. Let it come up to room temperature before using.

Winter vegetable soup

As the seasons change so does the selection of veggies in the shops, and we turn to chunky, warming soups with a hint of spice. This one is like a cosy overcoat, full of tasty goodness. We've suggested a selection of winter veg here, but feel free to use whatever root vegetables and greens you have available on the day. The chorizo really adds some oomph – we like the spicy version labelled picante.

Serves 6

2 tbsp vegetable oil

1 onion, finely sliced

3 garlic cloves, finely sliced

2 carrots

2 turnips

1 large potato (preferably Maris Piper)

1 large parsnip

2 heaped tsp sweet smoked paprika, plus extra to serve

1 heaped tsp hot smoked paprika

400g can of chopped tomatoes

1 tbsp tomato purée

125g chorizo sausage, skinned and cut into 5mm slices

100g Puy lentils, rinsed

1.75 litres chicken stock

100g cavolo nero, kale or spring greens, tough stems removed, shredded

soured cream or crème fraiche, to serve

sea salt and black pepper

Heat the oil in a large pan and fry the onion and garlic gently for 5 minutes, or until softened but not coloured, stirring occasionally. Cut the carrots, turnips, potato and parsnip into rough chunks of about 1.5cm.

Add the veg to the onion and garlic and cook over a low heat for 5 minutes, or until they are beginning to soften, stirring occasionally. Stir in both the sweet and hot paprikas and fry for a few minutes. Add the tomatoes and the tomato purée, turn up the heat a little and cook for another few minutes, stirring regularly.

Add the chorizo, lentils and the stock and bring to the boil. Reduce the heat and simmer the soup gently for 45 minutes, or until the vegetables and lentils are tender, stirring every now and then.

Add the cavolo nero, kale or spring greens to the pan and cook for 5 minutes or until softened. Season with salt and pepper and serve in deep bowls with a dollop of soured cream or crème fraiche and a sprinkling of paprika.

Waldorf salad

Our adventures over the past 20 years or so have taken us to some great hotels – including, would you believe, The Waldorf in New York! There we treated ourselves to big bowls of the creamy, crunchy deliciousness known as the Waldorf salad. The story is that it was first invented way back in 1896 by a chef at the NY Waldorf to serve at a charity ball. Whatever its origins, this has become a classic here in the UK as well as in the US and we think it's just right for a light lunch or as an accompaniment to some grilled chicken or meat.

Serves 4

Mayonnaise

2 egg yolks
1 tbsp white wine vinegar
2 tsp Dijon mustard
½ tsp caster sugar
¼ tsp flaked sea salt
150ml sunflower oil
100ml crème fraiche
black pepper

Waldorf salad

65g shelled walnut halves
3 large celery sticks, finely sliced and leaves reserved
2 eating apples, quartered and finely sliced
250g seedless red grapes, halved
about 2 tsp fresh lemon juice

To make the mayonnaise put the egg yolks, vinegar, mustard and sugar into the small bowl of a food processor, or use a bowl and a stick blender. Season with salt and some black pepper.

Blend until smooth, then, with the motor running, gradually add the oil and blend until smooth and thick. Add the crème fraiche and 1–2 tablespoons of cold water. Blend for a few seconds more until the sauce has a soft dropping consistency. Spoon into a bowl, cover and chill in the fridge.

For the salad, place the walnut halves in a small frying pan over a medium-high heat for a few minutes until nicely toasted, tossing them regularly. Remove the pan from the heat and leave the nuts to cool.

Add the sliced celery to a large bowl with the apples and grapes. Pour over the lemon juice and toss well. This will keep the apples from going brown. Mix in the mayonnaise, toasted walnut halves and celery leaves, then serve.

Roast squash salad

This is a good salad to make in winter when tomatoes are tasteless and lettuces are pricey. We came up with this idea for one of our Christmas programmes but, like puppies and kittens, it's not just for Christmas! The mixture of textures in this salad, with the meltingly soft squash and the crunchy pumpkin seeds and spinach leaves make it a real winner. Hope you agree.

Serves 4

———

½ large squash, peeled and seeded

2 tbsp olive oil

1 tsp dried thyme

3 garlic cloves, crushed

150g baby leaf spinach or similar young salad leaves (such as beetroot leaves)

50g pumpkin seeds

sea salt and black pepper

Dressing

2 tbsp olive oil

1 tbsp sherry vinegar

½ tsp runny honey

½ tsp wholegrain mustard

Preheat the oven to 200°C/180°C Fan/Gas 6. Cut the squash flesh into fairly small dice and put it all in a roasting tin. Toss with the oil, thyme and garlic, then season generously. Roast for 30 minutes, or until the squash has softened and is well browned around the edges. Allow to cool slightly.

Whisk together the dressing ingredients in large bowl.

Add the salad leaves to the dressing, season with salt and pepper, then toss lightly. Arrange the leaves on a serving dish. Toss the squash in the same bowl to pick up any remaining dressing, then arrange it over the salad leaves. Sprinkle with the pumpkin seeds and serve.

Hairy Biker tip: You can use the seeds from your squash instead of buying a packet of pumpkin seeds. Pull the seeds out of the central membrane and wash them to get rid of any orange flesh or tendrils, then dry them thoroughly. Heat a tablespoon of oil in a large frying pan and add the seeds. Fry them, shaking and stirring regularly until the seeds have taken on some colour and are releasing their aroma. Remove the seeds from the pan and leave them to cool. Season well with salt.

Caesar salad

Who doesn't love a great Caesar salad? It was recently voted the nation's favourite salad, though we have to say it has more to do with Las Vegas than Julius. We've added chicken to our recipe, but you could throw in some cooked prawns instead if you like, or just keep the salad simple and classic. The key to a Caesar salad is the little bit of magic that happens with the bringing together of Parmesan, anchovy, egg yolk and crunchy croutons. This salad makes a great filling for a wrap too.

Serves 4

Chicken (optional)

2 boneless, skinless chicken breasts

2 tbsp olive oil

juice of ½ lemon

1 tsp dried oregano or thyme

sea salt and black pepper

Croutons

½ ciabatta loaf, cut into cubes

4 tbsp olive oil

1 garlic clove, crushed

Dressing

6 anchovy fillets, finely chopped

juice of ½ lemon

1 tsp white wine vinegar

1 tsp Dijon mustard

4 tbsp olive oil

Salad

1 garlic clove, cut in half

2 romaine lettuce hearts, torn up

25g Parmesan cheese, grated

1 egg yolk

First prepare the chicken breasts, if using. Place a chicken breast on your work surface. Take a sharp knife and insert it along the long side of the breast. Slice into the breast, but stop just short of the other side. Open out the breast like a book. Repeat with the other chicken breast.

Put the olive oil, lemon juice and oregano or thyme into a bowl and season with salt and pepper. Add the chicken breasts and leave them to marinate for 30 minutes. Heat a griddle pan over a high heat until it is too hot to hold your hand over comfortably, then add the chicken. Griddle the breasts on each side for 3–4 minutes until they are completely cooked through and have deep char lines. Remove the chicken from the griddle, then when it's cool enough to handle, cut or tear it into strips.

To make the croutons, put the cubes of bread in a bowl and toss them with the olive oil until coated. Season with salt and pepper. Put the bread in a frying pan and sauté over a medium-hot heat, stirring regularly until it is all crisp and brown. When the bread is crisp enough, add the garlic and cook for another couple of minutes.

For the dressing, mash the anchovies into the lemon juice, vinegar and mustard. Drizzle in the olive oil, whisking constantly until the mixture thickens. Season with salt and pepper to taste.

To assemble the salad, take the garlic halves and rub them around the inside of a salad bowl. Add the lettuce, the chicken, if using, and the croutons. Sprinkle the Parmesan into the bowl and pour over the dressing. Drop the egg yolk on to the salad and toss thoroughly until the dressing, egg yolk and Parmesan have clung to the rest of the ingredients. Serve immediately.

Prawn cocktail

We've given this timeless classic a bit of a boost with some fiery Tabasco and a hit of chilli. A bit retro maybe, but we love a good prawn cocktail and always have done. *Dave*: I can still remember having my first prawn cocktail. It was on a trip to the TT races on the Isle of Man in 1966 with mum and dad. We ate at the Hotel Metropole and I had prawn cocktail followed by braised steak with a bay leaf on top. *Si*: The tradition in our household was to have prawn cocktail before the turkey every Christmas as a massive treat – and we still do!

Serves 4

———

500g frozen
　　Atlantic prawns,
　　defrosted and drained

150ml ready-made
　　gazpacho

150ml crème fraiche

1 shallot, very finely diced

2 tomatoes, skinned
　　and diced

1 red chilli, finely diced

6 radishes, finely sliced

small bunch of fresh
　　coriander, chopped

juice and zest of 1 lime

8 dashes of Tabasco

sea salt and black pepper

To serve

2 baby gem lettuces,
　　shredded

1 ripe avocado, peeled,
　　stoned and flesh sliced

4 pinches of
　　cayenne pepper

4 large cooked prawns,
　　heads and shells on

4 fresh coriander sprigs

Mix together the prawns, gazpacho, crème fraiche, shallot, tomatoes, chilli, radishes, coriander, lime juice and zest in a bowl until well combined. Season with the Tabasco and add salt and black pepper to taste.

Divide the shredded lettuce between your serving dishes. Arrange the avocado slices on top, then spoon over the prawn cocktail mixture. Sprinkle with cayenne pepper and garnish each serving with a prawn and a sprig of coriander.

Goats' cheese and chive soufflés

There's such a great range of British goats' cheese now and this dish really celebrates them. Our advice is don't be scared of soufflés. They're not that difficult to make and they look dead impressive served up as a starter or perhaps for lunch with a bit of salad. These little numbers are as light as cloud but a whole lot tastier.

Serves 4

50g butter, plus extra
    for greasing
3 tbsp grated Parmesan
    cheese
300ml whole milk
1 onion, quartered
1 bay leaf
1 small bunch of thyme
50g plain flour
200g goats' cheese,
    cut into 2cm pieces
4 eggs, separated
3 tbsp finely
    snipped chives
sea salt and black pepper

Butter the insides of 4 ramekins and sprinkle with about a tablespoon of the grated Parmesan. Put the milk in a small pan and add the onion, bay and thyme. Bring the milk to a gentle simmer, then remove from the heat and leave to infuse for 15 minutes.

Place a baking tray in the oven to heat up. Strain the flavoured milk through a fine sieve into a jug. Melt the butter in a heavy-based pan over a low heat. Stir in the flour and cook for a few seconds, then gradually start adding the milk, a little at a time, stirring well in between each addition. When the sauce is smooth and very thick, continue to cook for another couple of minutes, stirring constantly. Remove the pan from the heat and stir in half the goats' cheese.

Whisk the egg yolks lightly and stir them into the milk mixture until smooth. Season to taste with salt and pepper. Pour the mixture into a large bowl and cover the surface with cling film to prevent a skin forming. Preheat the oven to 220°C/Fan 200°C/Gas 7.

Whisk the egg whites with a pinch of salt until stiff but not dry. They are ready when you can turn the bowl upside down without them sliding out.

Stir the chives into the cheese sauce, then fold in the remaining cheese. Fold in a large spoonful of the egg white until combined, then fold in the rest. Pour the mixture slowly into the prepared dishes. Sprinkle with black pepper and the rest of the Parmesan, keeping it towards the centre of the soufflés so it doesn't melt and hinder the rise by sticking to the sides.

Place the dishes on the preheated baking tray and bake for about 15 minutes or until golden-brown and risen. Remove from the oven and serve the soufflés immediately.

Devilled whitebait with green sauce

Whitebait has long been a British classic. Charles Dickens himself used to go down to Greenwich on many an evening to enjoy a whitebait supper. Some years ago we enjoyed a dish of devilled whitebait in a seaside pub. Nothing flash – they came wrapped in brown paper – but so good. Try this and see if you agree. We think it is a real stand-out recipe and definitely one we wanted to share with you.

Serves 4
as a starter

———

750ml vegetable oil

6 tbsp plain flour

3 tbsp semolina

1 tsp English mustard powder

½ tsp cayenne pepper

400g whitebait, thawed if frozen

lemon wedges, to serve

Green sauce

2 large egg yolks

1 tbsp white wine vinegar

2 tsp Dijon mustard

½ tsp caster sugar

½ tsp sea salt, plus extra to season

150ml vegetable oil

1 small shallot, quartered

1 small garlic clove

1 tbsp baby capers, drained

15g parsley leaves

15g fresh sorrel or basil leaves

10g fresh mint leaves

10g tarragon leaves

1 tsp fresh lemon juice

black pepper

To make the green sauce, put the egg yolks, vinegar, mustard and sugar into the small bowl of a food processor. Don't use a large processor or the sauce won't combine properly. Season with half a teaspoon of salt and some black pepper.

Blitz until well combined then, with the motor running, very gradually pour the oil in a very thin stream on to the eggs and blend until smooth and thick. Add the shallot, garlic, capers, all the herbs and lemon juice and blend again until they are finely chopped and the sauce is very green. If you don't have a food processor, you could use a jug and a stick blender. Adjust the seasoning to taste and add a tablespoon of cold water. Blend for a few seconds more until the sauce has a soft spoonable consistency, adding a little more water if necessary. Spoon the sauce into a serving bowl.

Pour the oil into a large pan or a deep-fat fryer and heat to 180°C. Check the temperature with a cooking thermometer.

Put the flour, semolina, mustard powder and cayenne pepper in a large bowl. Season with lots of black pepper and mix well. Put the whitebait in a colander and rinse them under cold water, then drain.

When the oil is at the right temperature, take a quarter of the damp whitebait and toss them with the seasoned flour. Lift them out with a slotted spoon and give them a quick shake to dislodge some of the excess flour – they need to be lightly coated. The fish shouldn't be too dry or the flour won't stick, so rinse them in more water and drain again if necessary.

Lower the floured fish gently into the oil and fry them for 2½ minutes until they are crisp and golden. Stir once towards the end of the cooking time to separate the fish. Remove the fish with a slotted spoon and drain them on kitchen paper. Scoop out any scraps of fish that remain and bring the oil back to 180°C. Cook the rest of the fish, then serve them with the sauce and some lemon wedges.

Squid with chilli and garlic dipping sauce

More and more squid is being caught in British waters now and it's really good. People say it might even replace cod as your favourite fish supper so don't be squeamish about squid! We always order this dish when we see it on a menu but it's so easy to make at home too. Frozen squid is cheap and convenient, as it's all cleaned and ready to go. What's more, freezing tenderises the squid, making it even more delicious.

Serves 4

2 x 175–200g whole
   prepared squid

2 heaped tsp Sichuan
   peppercorns

2 heaped tsp black
   peppercorns

½ tsp dried chilli flakes

1 tbsp flaked sea salt

5 tbsp self-raising flour

5 tbsp cornflour

vegetable oil, for
   shallow frying

Dipping sauce

100g caster sugar

2 tbsp white wine vinegar

1 long red chilli,
   finely chopped

2 garlic cloves, finely
   chopped

15g fresh root ginger,
   peeled and finely
   chopped

1 tbsp chopped
   fresh coriander

For the dipping sauce, put the sugar and a tablespoon of the vinegar in a small pan with 50ml of water and heat gently until the sugar dissolves, stirring constantly. Bring to the boil and cook for 1 minute. Add the chilli, garlic and ginger and cook for a further minute, stirring occasionally. Remove the pan from the heat, stir in the remaining vinegar and leave to cool.

Cut the squid pieces along one side and open them out. Score the insides with a criss-cross pattern using the tip of a knife, working diagonally across the flesh. Cut the tentacles into quarters, then set all the squid aside.

Put the peppercorns, chilli flakes and salt in a small pan and heat them gently until you can smell the peppery aromas. Tip everything into a mortar and pound hard with a pestle until the mixture has the texture of freshly ground black pepper. Tip this into a bowl and stir in the self-raising flour and cornflour.

Add the squid to the bowl and mix until the squid is well coated with the spiced flour. Set aside while the oil is heating. Stir the coriander into the cooled dipping sauce and pour into a small bowl.

Pour 2cm of oil into a pan, place it over a medium heat and heat to 180°C. Be warned: hot oil can be dangerous so never leave it unattended.

When the oil reaches the right temperature, drop in a few pieces of the squid, adding it a piece at a time, so it doesn't clump together. Fry for 1–2 minutes until the squid is pale golden-brown and crisp, then remove and drain it on kitchen paper. Cook the rest in the same way, allowing the oil to get back to the right temperature each time.

Serve the fried squid with the dipping sauce.

Pork and pistachio pâté

Also known as mortadella mousse and dead easy to make. Sometimes when we're travelling we come across a new dish that we just can't wait to cook, and this tasty pâté topped with pistachios is one of those. It's a new classic made with that Italian sausage called mortadella that you see on every supermarket deli counter. *Dave*: When I was on my holidays in Italy a year or so ago I ate a version of this in a posh restaurant, then another a couple of days later in a little café. Both were amazing and it was the first thing I cooked when I got home.

Serves 4–6

————

12 slices of
   mortadella sausage
50ml crème fraiche
100ml double cream
75g Parmesan cheese,
   finely grated
pinch of freshly
   grated nutmeg
sea salt and black pepper

To serve
2 tbsp pistachios,
   lightly crushed
rounds of bread
butter, for spreading
   (optional)

Put the mortadella in a food processor and blend until it is finely chopped. Add the crème fraiche and half the cream, then continue to blend.

Add the grated Parmesan and blend again. Gradually add the remaining cream, blending all the time, until you have a smooth paste. Season with the nutmeg and black pepper to taste – you may not want to add salt.

Scrape the mixture into a bowl and smooth the top. Sprinkle over the pistachios.

Toast the bread and spread it with butter if you like. Serve the pâté on the toast.

Pork and chicken terrine

A terrine looks really fancy and impressive but actually isn't that difficult to make. This beautiful parsley-flecked pork and chicken number makes a great dinner party starter – and it's just as good eaten with a bag of crisps in front of the telly. It's nice at any time of year – useful to have in the fridge over Christmas to serve to hungry visitors and also perfect for packing into a summer picnic basket. Make this the day before you want to eat it.

Serves 6–8

_____

Chicken layer

200g boneless, skinless
   chicken breasts

100ml white wine

zest of 1 lemon

leaves from 1 thyme sprig

1 tbsp olive oil

4 tbsp finely
   chopped parsley

sea salt and black pepper

Pork layers

300g trimmed pork
   shoulder

300g rindless pork belly

zest of 1 lemon

1 tbsp thyme leaves,
   finely chopped

¼ tsp ground ginger

75g dried apricots,
   finely chopped

25g pistachio kernels,
   halved

To assemble

400g streaky bacon
   rashers, rinds removed

Slice the chicken breasts into strips. Place them in a bowl, season and add the white wine, zest and thyme. Drizzle over the oil, cover and leave the chicken to marinate for at least an hour.

For the pork layers, finely chop the pork shoulder and pork belly, or put the whole lot through a meat grinder, or blend in a food processor. Put it all in a bowl with the lemon zest, thyme, ginger, apricots and pistachios and mix well. Season with salt and pepper.

Preheat the oven to 150°C/Fan 130°C/Gas 2. Stretch the bacon rashers with the back of the knife, then use some of them to line a 1-litre terrine mould or a loaf tin. Place them widthways, arranging them on alternate diagonals so that they overlap and hang over the sides of the mould or tin. Stretch the bacon out a little more if you need to.

Put half the pork mixture into the terrine and spread it evenly. Remove the chicken from the marinade and mix it with the chopped parsley, then lay the strips out in an even layer over the pork. Cover with the remaining pork mixture.

Cover the top of the terrine with the overhanging bacon slices, then top with more slices of bacon so that it is completely covered.

Put the lid on the terrine or cover it with a double layer of foil. Place it in a roasting tin and add just enough boiled water to reach up to 2cm up the sides. Put it in the oven and bake for 1½ hours.

To check if the terrine is cooked through, test it with a meat probe or thermometer – it should reach 75°C. Alternatively, just hold a skewer in the centre for a few seconds – if the tip is too hot to hold for more than a second, the terrine is done. Cover the terrine with a double layer of foil, then weigh it down with a couple of tins or something else heavy. Leave to cool, then put it in the fridge overnight. To serve, turn the terrine out and cut it into thick slices.

Mini toad in the holes

We've given you toad in the hole recipes in the past and we've been trying to think how to make this awesome favourite even better. Well, we're pleased to tell you that we can. Slicing the sausage really helps maximise the flavour and we think these mini versions – you could call them tadpoles in the hole – make perfect starters or canapés if you're feeling fancy. Kids love them too. And if you're mega hungry, just eat three!

Makes 8–12

1 heaped tbsp lard or
    goose or duck fat
1 large onion, sliced
8 pork sausages
sea salt

Batter
150g plain flour
1 tsp dried sage
2 eggs, beaten
275ml whole milk

First make the batter. Put the flour into a bowl and whisk it lightly to get rid of any lumps, then add a generous pinch of salt and the dried sage. Make a well in the middle and add the eggs. Work the eggs into the flour, then gradually add the milk. Alternatively, put everything in a food processor and blitz until smooth. Leave the batter to stand for an hour.

Preheat the oven to 200°C/Fan 180°C/Gas 6. Divide the lard or goose or duck fat between 2 x 4-hole Yorkshire pudding tins or 1 x 12 hole tin. Put the tins in the oven to heat up.

Bring a small pan of water to the boil. Add a pinch of salt and the onion slices. Simmer them for 3 minutes, then drain thoroughly. Cut the sausages into rounds. Divide the onion and sausages between the tins.

Put the tins back in the oven and cook for 20 minutes, until the sausages have started to look nice and brown.

Remove the tins from the oven. Pour in the batter around the sausages and onion – there should be just enough batter to reach the top of each hole. Bake for a further 20 minutes until the Yorkshire puddings have risen and are a dark golden-brown. Serve hot straight from the oven – with some gravy if you like.

FAVOURITE FAMILY SUPPERS

Vegetable garden risotto 50

Spiced roasted cauliflower cheese 52

Glamorgan sausages with red onion and chilli relish 54

Pan haggerty 56

Homity pie 58

Ploughman's fondue AKA The Ploughdoo 60

Fishcakes with parsley sauce 62

Mussels à la Biker 66

Crab and leek tart 68

Fish fillets with tarragon sauce 70

Cumberland sausage, chicken and squash tray bake 72

Meatloaf with gravy 74

Swedish meatballs 76

Mince and herby dumplings 78

Hand-rolled spinach pasta with paprika meatballs 80

Easy Biker lasagne 82

Vegetable garden risotto

For many people, including us, risotto is a go-to supper dish throughout the year. This recipe, featuring lots of beautiful British veggies, is perfect for the spring, when asparagus makes its first appearance, although it's fine to use frozen peas and beans if you like. The cheese really lifts the flavour and the minted oil adds the finishing touch. If making this for two, just half the quantity of rice and liquid and add the amount of veg you want.

Serves 4

250g podded fresh or
  frozen broad beans

50g butter

1 tbsp olive oil

1 onion, finely chopped

2 garlic cloves, crushed

3–4 thyme sprigs

1 long strip of lemon zest

1 bay leaf

150g risotto rice

150ml dry white wine

750ml hot vegetable stock

100g fresh runner beans,
  cut into long thin strips

100g podded fresh or
  frozen peas

1 bunch of asparagus,
  cut into short lengths

100g feta cheese, drained
  and crumbled

sea salt and black pepper

Parmesan shavings,
  to serve (optional)

Minted olive oil

1 tbsp chopped
  fresh mint leaves

2 tbsp olive oil

To make the minted oil, mix the mint and olive oil, then set it aside.

Bring a pan of water to the boil, add the broad beans and bring back to the boil, then cook for 1 minute. Drain the beans and run them under cold water to cool, then remove their greyish skins and set aside.

Melt 25g of the butter with the tablespoon of oil in a large pan and fry the onion for a few minutes until softened, but not coloured. Add the garlic and cook for another couple of minutes, then stir in the thyme, lemon zest, bay leaf and rice and cook for a few seconds longer until the rice is glistening.

Pour the wine into the pan and cook over a medium heat until the liquid has reduced by half. Slowly start adding the stock, a ladleful at a time, stirring well in between each addition. Simmer for 2–3 minutes or until the liquid has almost all been absorbed before adding more. Continue to cook and add stock for 15 minutes or until the rice is tender.

Meanwhile, bring a separate pan of water to the boil. Add the runner beans and cook them for 3 minutes, or until tender. Drain, then tip the beans back into the pan and toss with a small knob of butter and plenty of pepper.

Remove the thyme and lemon zest from the rice and discard. Stir in the broad beans, peas and asparagus with the remaining stock and cook for 3 minutes until tender, stirring regularly. Remove from the heat and stir in the feta. Season with salt and pepper, then cover with a lid and set aside for a few moments.

Add the remaining butter to the risotto and stir. Serve, topped with some runner beans, minted olive oil and shavings of Parmesan, if using.

Spiced roasted cauliflower cheese

Cauliflower has featured in our cooking for as long as we can remember. We've roasted it, riced it, made it into pizza bases, everything you can think of, but we always come back to good old cauliflower cheese. Quite simply, it's a brilliant supper dish and everyone loves it. In this new version the strong, earthy flavour of the cauli marries well with the spices, and roasting it makes it even tastier. Cauli cheese tends to be a stand-alone dish these days, but we both have fond memories of it as an accompaniment to a Sunday roast.

Serves 4

1 large cauliflower, separated into florets

glug of extra virgin olive oil

1 tsp salt

1 tsp ground black pepper

1 tsp ground cumin

2 tsp ground paprika

1 tsp fennel seeds, crushed

1 red chilli, seeds removed, chopped

2 tsp honey

4 tsp lemon juice

zest of 1 lemon

100g Emmental cheese, grated

50g Gruyère cheese, grated

Preheat the oven to 190°C/Fan 170°C Fan/Gas 5.

Bring a pan of salted water to the boil. Add the cauliflower florets, bring the water back to the boil and cook for 5 minutes. Drain and tip the florets into a large mixing bowl. Add the olive oil, salt, pepper, cumin, paprika and fennel seeds and stir to coat the blanched florets thoroughly. Add the chilli, honey and lemon juice. Stir to coat the cauliflower with the mixture again, taking care to keep the florets intact.

Place all the cauliflower in a large ovenproof dish and roast in the oven for 15 minutes or so until golden-brown. Remove the dish from the oven and sprinkle over the lemon zest and then the cheese. Put the dish back in the oven and roast until the cheese is bubbling and has a little colour. Serve at once.

Glamorgan sausages with red onion and chilli relish

We were challenged to make a great veggie sausage so we looked to the traditional Glamorgan sausage for inspiration. This is our version with a great spicy relish that goes with the sausages as perfectly as – did we hear you say, Si and Dave? Get away with you! Mini versions are nice for party snacks too.

Serves 4

—————

25g butter

115g leeks (prepared weight), finely sliced

175g fresh white breadcrumbs

2 tbsp chopped fresh parsley

1 tbsp chopped fresh thyme

150g Cheddar cheese, finely grated

2 eggs, separated

1 tsp English mustard

½ tsp sea salt

5 tbsp vegetable oil

black pepper

Red onion and chilli relish

2 tbsp vegetable oil

2 medium red onions, finely sliced

1 red chilli, finely chopped

2 garlic cloves, crushed

75g light brown muscovado sugar

5 tbsp white wine vinegar

Melt the butter in a frying pan and fry the slices of leek gently for about 10 minutes, or until very soft but not coloured.

Put 100g of the breadcrumbs with the parsley, thyme and cheese in a large bowl and mix until well combined. Beat the egg yolks with the mustard, salt and plenty of pepper in a separate bowl.

Remove the frying pan from the heat and add the leeks to the breadcrumb mixture. Add the egg yolks and mix until well combined. Divide the leek mixture into 8 and roll into sausage shapes, placing them on a baking tray lined with cling film.

Lightly whisk the egg whites in a bowl until just frothy. Sprinkle 40g of the remaining breadcrumbs over a large plate. Dip the sausages, one at a time, into the beaten egg white, then roll them in the breadcrumbs until evenly coated and place them on the baking tray. Put the sausages in the fridge to firm up for 30 minutes.

For the relish, heat the 2 tablespoons of oil in a pan and fry the onions for 20 minutes, or until very soft and just beginning to colour. Add the chilli and garlic and cook for a further 5 minutes, stirring regularly. Sprinkle with the sugar and pour over the vinegar. Bring to a simmer and cook for another 5 minutes, or until the liquid is well reduced and the relish is thick and glossy. Remove the pan from the heat and allow the relish to cool for a few minutes, then tip it into a bowl.

Heat the 5 tablespoons oil in a large frying pan and fry the sausages over a medium heat for 10–12 minutes, until they're golden-brown and crisp, turning them regularly. Serve the sausages with the relish and some veg.

Hairy Biker tip: If you want a milder relish, use just half a chilli. Up to you whether you remove the seeds – keeping the seeds makes the relish hotter.

Pan haggerty

We cooked this classic Northumbrian one-pot wonder on our 'Mums Know Best' series because Stella, Si's mam, made the best pan haggerty ever. It proved to be a huge success with the viewers and we've cooked it ever since in a quest to make it even better. Nothing like it for warming you up on a cold evening.

Serves 6

——————

1 tbsp vegetable oil

250g streaky bacon

6 potatoes, thinly sliced into rounds

2 onions, sliced

5 carrots, sliced

500ml chicken stock

150g Cheddar cheese, grated

crusty bread, to serve

sea salt and black pepper, to taste

Heat the vegetable oil in a deep ovenproof pan. Fry the bacon rashers for 3–4 minutes, or until golden-brown and slightly crisp. Remove them from the pan and set aside to drain on kitchen paper.

Arrange a layer of the sliced potatoes in the bottom of the pan. Cover them with a layer of sliced onions, then a layer of sliced carrots. Layer over some of the crisp bacon, then season with salt and pepper.

Repeat the process with the remaining potatoes, onions, carrots and bacon, finishing with a layer of potatoes. Season with salt and black pepper.

Pour in the chicken stock to cover the ingredients, then bring to the boil. Cover the pan with a lid and reduce the heat to a simmer. Simmer for 15–25 minutes, or until the potatoes and carrots are tender. Preheat the grill to high.

Uncover the pan and sprinkle over the grated cheese. Put the pan under a preheated grill for 5–6 minutes, or until the cheese is bubbling and golden-brown.

Serve the pan haggerty with some crusty bread to mop up the juices.

Homity pie

Popular in the seventies and eighties, homity pies were often seen as somewhat worthy – leathery, unappetising with a smug crust. But we thought this pie deserved a second look. This recipe is the grandson of those early pies and, we bashfully believe, a great improvement. We've cut down on the potatoes to make it less heavy and added some broccoli and other root veg – although you can vary these as you like. Celeriac and swede would also work well. A great veggie dish that can be enjoyed by all.

Serves 4–6

400g waxy potatoes, diced

300g carrots, diced

150g turnips, diced

200g small broccoli florets

15g butter

2 onions, thickly sliced

2 garlic cloves, finely chopped

175g Cheddar cheese, grated

2 tbsp finely chopped parsley

50ml milk or water

1 tsp Dijon mustard

200ml double cream

sea salt

Pastry

125g plain flour

125g wholemeal flour

150g cold butter, diced

1 egg, beaten

To make the pastry, put the flours and butter into a food processor with a generous pinch of salt and pulse until the mixture resembles breadcrumbs. Add the egg and just enough cold water to bind the mixture together. Shape the dough into a ball, wrap it in cling film, and leave it to chill in the fridge while you make the filling.

Bring a large saucepan of water to the boil. Add the potatoes, carrots and turnips and bring the water back to the boil. Cook for 4 minutes, then add the broccoli. Continue to cook until the vegetables are just done but still with a little bite to them – this will take about another 2 minutes. Drain and leave to cool.

While the vegetables are cooking, melt the butter in a large frying pan. Add the onions with a pinch of salt and cook, stirring regularly, until the onions have softened and are lightly coloured. Add the garlic and continue to cook for another 2 minutes. Remove the pan from the heat and set aside to cool. Preheat the oven to 200°C/Fan 180°C/Gas 6.

Put all the cooled vegetables into a large bowl. Add 100g of the cheese and the parsley, then mix thoroughly and set aside.

Roll out the pastry and use it to line a 20cm cake tin or a deep pie dish. Spoon the filling over the pastry. Whisk the milk and mustard together until you have a thin paste, then stir this into the cream. Season with a little salt. Pour this mixture in a slow and steady stream over the filling so it soaks through the layers of vegetables. Sprinkle the remaining cheese on top.

Bake the pie in the oven for 40–45 minutes until the pastry is crisp and lightly coloured and the cheese has melted and started to brown. Serve hot or at room temperature.

Ploughman's fondue AKA The Ploughdoo

More Shropshire than Switzerland, this takes the retro joy of the fondue and livens it up with the addition of some great British ale and cheese. Then just get yourself loads of veg, pickles and cubes of crusty bread and start dipping. As we like to say, 'How do, let's have a ploughdoo!'

Serves 4

250g mature Cheddar
   cheese, grated

2 tbsp cornflour

1 tsp English
   mustard powder

1 small garlic clove, peeled

200ml pale ale

To serve

small pickled onions,
   drained

cubes of crusty bread,
   such as sourdough,
   baguette, wholegrain
   or rye

cherry tomatoes,
   radishes, celery sticks,
   baby gem lettuce leaves,
   spring onions

farmhouse pickle

Mix the grated Cheddar with the cornflour and mustard powder in a bowl.

Rub the garlic clove vigorously around the inside of a pan – a cast-iron saucepan is ideal – or a fondue pot. Pour the beer into the pan and bring it to a very gentle simmer over a low heat.

Add the cheese mixture, a handful at a time, stirring well and allowing it to melt before adding more. It is important to keep stirring once the cheese is added.

Simmer gently for 3 minutes, stirring constantly until the fondue looks smooth and glossy. Add a little extra ale if the cheese mixture is any thicker than a pourable custard. Transfer to a burner and keep warm while the fondue is served.

Arrange all the dipping ingredients on a board and put the pickle in a dish.

Then have fun dipping the pickled onions, bread and vegetables into the melted cheese. Add a little pickle to each serving if you like. If the cheese thickens a little too much while you're eating, add a tablespoon or so of just-boiled water and stir well.

Fishcakes with parsley sauce

This recipe might look a bit long but please don't be put off. All the steps are simple, the end result is perfect and we knew we couldn't possibly have a book on British classics without a great fishcake. We like plenty of fish in our fishcakes and using three different types really is worth it – the salmon adds a touch of luxury and a different texture to the white fish, while the smoked haddock brings a special flavour. Parsley sauce is an essential accompaniment we reckon, and it's a handy recipe to know, as it goes with many types of fish.

Serves 6

———

600g potatoes (preferably Maris Pipers), cut into chunks

250g thick cod fillet, unskinned

250g thick salmon fillet, unskinned

100g smoked haddock fillet, unskinned

500ml whole milk

1 bay leaf

grated zest of ½ lemon

6 spring onions, trimmed and finely sliced

25g plain flour, for dusting

2 eggs

100g fresh white breadcrumbs

75ml vegetable oil

lemon wedges, for serving

sea salt and black pepper

Parsley sauce

25g butter

25g plain flour

reserved milk from cooking the fish

25g curly leaf parsley, finely chopped

Put the potatoes in a pan of cold water and bring to the boil. Cook for 12–15 minutes, or until the potatoes are soft but not falling apart. Drain the potatoes and mash until smooth, then season well. Spread the mash out on a cold plate and leave to cool.

Place the fish in a large saucepan, with the thicker fillets at the bottom of the pan. Pour the milk into the pan, add the bay leaf and season with a little salt and some pepper.

Cover the pan with a tight-fitting lid and gently bring to a simmer. Immediately, take the pan off the heat and leave it to stand for 10 minutes. This will finish cooking the fish and infuse the milk with flavour.

Remove the fish from the milk and transfer the fillets to a plate. Set the milk aside to make the parsley sauce. Break the fish into large chunks, discarding the skin as you go. Leave the fish to cool completely.

Place the cooled mash in a large bowl and stir in the lemon zest and spring onions. Tip the cooled fish into the mash and use a wooden spoon to mix it into the mash, without breaking up the fish too much.

Divide the mixture into 6 balls. Flatten each ball until it is about 3cm thick and place the flattened balls on a baking tray lined with baking paper. Put the tray in the freezer for about 20 minutes or in the fridge for 45 minutes to firm up the fishcakes.

To coat the fishcakes, sprinkle the flour for dusting over a plate. Beat the eggs in a shallow bowl and spread half the breadcrumbs over a large plate.

Dip a fishcake into the flour, coating it well on all sides. Gently pat off any excess flour, then dip the fishcake into the egg, coating it on all sides. Allow any excess egg to drip off of the fishcake and then place it in the breadcrumbs. Turn the fishcake in the crumbs and press them firmly and evenly on to all the sides. Place the fishcake on a tray lined with baking paper and repeat until you've coated all the fishcakes, replacing the used crumbs with the reserved breadcrumbs for the final 3.

You can then leave the fishcakes in the fridge until you're ready to cook, but use them within 24 hours.

To cook the fishcakes, preheat the oven to 200°C/Fan 180°C/Gas 6. Heat the oil in a large frying pan. Place 3 of the fishcakes in the pan and fry them over a medium-high heat for 3 minutes on each side. Put them on a baking tray while you fry the rest, adding a little more oil to the pan if necessary.

Place the tray of fishcakes in the oven for 8–10 minutes to finish cooking. They should be hot throughout.

While the fishcakes are in the oven, make the parsley sauce. Melt the butter in a small pan. Gradually add the flour, stirring with a wooden spoon until the mixture comes away from the sides of the pan. Slowly add the reserved milk, stirring constantly with a wooden spoon to get rid of any lumps.

Bring the sauce to a simmer and cook for a few minutes, or until the sauce is thickened and smooth. Remove the pan from the heat and stir in the parsley. Season with salt and pepper to taste.

Serve the fishcakes with the parsley sauce and some lemon wedges for squeezing.

Mussels à la Biker

Mussels are regular favourites in both our households. They're plentiful, cheap and tasty and they make great dishes to share. You find mussels in the poshest restaurants and the most basic seaside caffs and they adapt well to many different cuisines. In this simple one-pot recipe, the mussels are flavoured with a little wine and a hint of saffron and chilli. Quick to make and a belting good dish.

Serves 4

1kg mussels

2 tbsp olive oil

15g butter

1 small onion, finely chopped

1 fennel bulb, roughly chopped, any fronds reserved

2 garlic cloves, finely chopped

150ml white wine

pinch of saffron

strip of orange zest

½ tsp chilli flakes

2 tomatoes, peeled and finely chopped

100ml fish or vegetable stock or water

handful of parsley, finely chopped, to garnish

sea salt and black pepper

First prepare the mussels. Wash them thoroughly, scraping off any barnacles and pulling out the beards. Discard any mussels with broken shells or any that do not close tightly when you tap them sharply.

Make the sauce. Heat the olive oil and butter in a large pan. Add the onion and fennel and cook them over a medium-low heat, stirring regularly, until they have softened and turned translucent.

Add the garlic and cook for a further couple of minutes, then pour in the wine. Add the saffron, orange zest and chilli flakes. Season with salt and pepper.

Bring to the boil, then turn the heat down and simmer for 5 minutes. Add the tomatoes and stock or water and continue to cook for another 5 minutes.

Add the mussels to the pan and cover with a lid. Leave them to cook for 3–4 minutes, giving the pan a good shake at intervals. The mussels are ready when they have completely opened. Discard any that remain closed.

Serve the mussels in shallow bowls with the sauce spooned over. Sprinkle with plenty of parsley and any reserved fennel fronds.

Hairy Biker tip: To skin tomatoes, make a small cross in the base of each tomato with the tip of a knife. Put the tomatoes in a heatproof bowl and cover with just-boiled water. Leave the tomatoes to stand for 30–60 seconds until the skins begin to wrinkle back, then drain. When the tomatoes are cool enough to handle, strip off the skins and chuck them away.

Crab and leek tart

Crab and leek are a perfect combo and they make a great tart. We know crab isn't cheap but it has a good strong flavour and you don't need a lot for this dish. We both have fond memories of going crabbing as kids. Dave: I used to go crabbing with my dad as soon as I could walk and hold a bucket. Si: I used to love going rock pooling with my mam and dad when we were on our holidays. We didn't catch much but it was fun trying.

Serves 6–8

Pastry

100g plain flour, plus extra for rolling

100g wholemeal flour

125g cold butter, cubed

1 egg, beaten

Filling

knob of butter

2 medium leeks, thinly sliced

3 eggs

300ml crème fraiche

100g fresh brown crab meat

100g fresh white crab meat

50g mature Cheddar, finely grated

sea salt and black pepper

For the pastry, pulse the flours and butter in a food processor until the mixture resembles fine breadcrumbs. With the motor running, add the egg in a thin stream and blend until the mixture begins to form a ball.

Roll the pastry into a circle on a floured work surface and use it to line a 23cm tart tin. Press the pastry with your fingertips firmly into the base and sides. Trim any excess pastry and lightly prick the base of the tart with a fork. Chill it in the fridge for 30 minutes. Preheat the oven to 200°C/Fan 180°C/Gas 6.

Line the pastry with baking paper and half fill it with baking beans. Bake the tart case for 25 minutes. Remove the beans and put the tart back in the oven for 5–10 minutes or until the surface is dry and beginning to brown. Remove from the oven and turn the oven down to 180°C/Fan 160°C/Gas 4.

Now make the filling. Melt the butter in a large frying pan over a low heat. Add the leeks and fry them gently for 2–3 minutes until just softened. Remove the pan from the heat and set it aside.

Beat the eggs in a bowl, then add the crème fraiche, season and beat together with a wooden spoon until thoroughly combined. Stir in the brown crab meat.

Scatter the leeks over the pastry case and dot the white crab meat around them. Pour over the crème fraiche and brown crab meat mixture, then sprinkle with the cheese. Cook the tart for 25 minutes, or until the filling is golden-brown and just set. The tart should still wobble a tiny bit in the centre as it will continue to set as it cools. Remove the tart from the oven and leave it to cool in the tin for 15 minutes before serving.

Fish fillets with tarragon sauce

Si: People often ask us if we ever fall out and no, we don't really. But there is one thing that we do differ on – very strongly as it happens: Dave hates fish on the bone – an autopsy on the plate he calls it – while I'm quite happy to cook whole fish. We do agree, though, that fish fillets are the ultimate fast food. They're a great thing to have in the freezer, ready for a quick meal. Try a fish fillet with this tasty sauce and you have a meal in no time. Tarragon makes a nice change from parsley and goes really well with fish and chicken. You'll find it in the supermarket but it's easy to grow in a pot on your kitchen windowsill.

Serves 4

4 fish fillets, such as sea bass or sea bream, skin on

1 tbsp olive oil

sea salt and black pepper

Tarragon sauce

15g butter

1 shallot, very finely chopped

100ml white wine

100ml fish, vegetable or chicken stock

finely grated zest of ½ lemon

300ml single cream

leaves from a small bunch of tarragon, finely chopped

1–2 tsp lemon juice, to taste

First make the sauce. Melt the butter in a small saucepan. Add the shallot and cook it over a low heat until it is very soft and translucent – it should almost melt into the butter.

Pour in the white wine and bring to the boil. Add the stock and continue to simmer until the liquid has reduced by half. Stir in the lemon zest, cream and tarragon and simmer for a further 5 minutes until the sauce has thickened enough to coat the back of your spoon.

Season with salt and pepper, then taste and add lemon juice to taste. Keep the sauce warm while you cook the fish.

Heat a large frying pan. Pat the fish fillets dry with kitchen paper, then season them lightly with salt and pepper. Heat the oil in the pan and add the fillets, skin-side down. Cook them for 4–5 minutes until the skin is crisp and comes away easily from the pan. Flip them over and cook them on the other side for a minute.

Serve the fish with the sauce and some nice veg.

Cumberland sausage, chicken and squash tray bake

Years ago at the top of Hardknott Pass in the Lake District we cooked chicken breasts stuffed with Cumberland sausages and that dish was our inspiration for this great tray bake. It's one of our very favourites so we had to include it here. Nothing like a tray bake for a good easy supper we always say, and this one has loads of great flavours brought to life by the addition of a touch of maple syrup and red wine vinegar. Cook a big pile of greens to go alongside and supper is a breeze.

Serves 4

4 chicken thighs,
   skin on, bone in

4–6 meaty pork sausages

500g pumpkin or squash,
   cut into wedges

2 onions, cut into wedges

a few thyme sprigs, or
   1 tsp dried thyme

2 tbsp olive oil

50ml red wine

1 tbsp maple syrup

1 tsp red wine vinegar

½ tsp chilli flakes
   (optional)

200g chestnut
   mushrooms, halved

sea salt and black pepper

Preheat the oven to 220°C/200°C Fan/Gas 7.

Put the chicken thighs, skin-side up, in a roasting tin with the sausages, pumpkin or squash and the onions. Season with salt and pepper, sprinkle over the thyme and drizzle a tablespoon of the oil over the top.

Mix the red wine with 100ml of water and pour this into the tin. Put the tin in the oven and roast for 30 minutes. Turn the sausages over halfway through cooking to help them brown nicely.

Mix the maple syrup with the red wine vinegar and drizzle it over the contents of the roasting tin. Sprinkle over the chilli flakes, if using. Add the mushrooms to the tin and drizzle with another tablespoon of olive oil.

Roast for another 25–30 minutes, or until everything is cooked through and well browned. Serve with any pan juices spooned over the top. Yum!

Meatloaf with gravy

A few years back we did some filming at Arnold's Country Kitchen in Nashville where we were behind the counter serving up their famous 'meat and 3' – meatloaf and three sides. We thought we would turn the idea round and make a British meatloaf with three different meats and we think it's the tastiest thing ever, a true classic. It's great hot with gravy but a slice of cold meatloaf would also be very welcome in a lunchbox.

Serves 6

————

1 tbsp vegetable oil

1 onion, finely chopped

1 carrot, diced

1 celery stick, trimmed
   and diced

2 garlic cloves, crushed

1–1½ tsp chilli powder

1 tsp dried thyme
   or 1 tbsp chopped
   fresh thyme

300g minced beef

300g minced pork

450g good-quality pork
   sausage meat

7 tbsp tomato ketchup

2 tbsp Worcestershire
   sauce

75g fresh white
   breadcrumbs

1 small bunch of flatleaf
   parsley, leaves chopped

1 egg, beaten

1 tsp fine sea salt

2 tbsp dark brown sugar

black pepper

Gravy

1 tbsp plain flour

400ml beef or pork stock

1 tsp ketchup

Heat the oil in a large frying pan and gently fry the onion, carrot and celery for 10 minutes until well softened, stirring regularly. Add the garlic, chilli powder and thyme and cook for a further 2 minutes, stirring constantly. Remove the pan from the heat and tip the contents into a bowl, then leave to cool for 10–15 minutes. Preheat the oven to 200°C/Fan 180°C/Gas 6.

Add the beef, pork, sausage meat, 3 tablespoons of the ketchup, a tablespoon of the Worcestershire sauce, the breadcrumbs, parsley, egg, salt and plenty of pepper to the vegetables. Mix with your hands until thoroughly combined – the mixture should be fairly stiff but moist.

Put the meatloaf mixture into a small roasting tin and shape it into a loaf measuring about 28 x 14cm. Mix the rest of the ketchup and Worcestershire sauce with the sugar and spread it over the top of the meatloaf.

Bake the meatloaf in the oven for 45 minutes until browned and firm. The loaf will release lots of juice as it cooks and you can use this to make the gravy. Remove the loaf from the oven and transfer it to a warmed plate. Cover it loosely with a piece of foil.

For the gravy, put the roasting tin on the hob over a low heat and stir in the flour with a wooden spoon. Cook for about 30 seconds, stirring constantly. Slowly start adding the stock, a little at a time, stirring until it is all incorporated. Add the teaspoon of ketchup.

Bring the gravy to a simmer and cook for 4–5 minutes, stirring to lift the juices and sticky bits from the base of the tin. Whisk to get rid of any lumps and season with a little more salt and pepper if you think it needs it. Strain the gravy through a sieve into a warmed jug. Cut the meatloaf into thick slices and serve with the gravy.

Swedish meatballs

A famous furniture retailer – you know who we mean – sells two million of these meatballs every day and they have become a British classic. Now you can forget queuing with a flat-pack wardrobe on your back and make your own Swedish meatballs and gravy at home. We cooked our version for our telly series on the Baltic and the Scandinavians thought they were sensational. We were really chuffed with them too and they were the first thing we cooked when we got home to the UK. Abba-tastic! By the way, lingonberry jam is a Swedish speciality made with wild berries similar to cranberries. If you can't find any, good old redcurrant jelly works fine.

Serves 4–6

1 tbsp olive oil

1 onion, finely chopped

1 garlic clove, finely chopped

600g pork or wild boar, minced

4 anchovy fillets, finely chopped

100g breadcrumbs

1 egg

50ml milk or single cream

½ tsp allspice

¼ tsp nutmeg

sea salt and black pepper

Gravy

25g butter

25g flour

100ml white wine

500ml beef stock

2 tbsp single cream

1 tbsp lingonberry jam or redcurrant jelly, plus extra to serve

To serve

a few dill sprigs, finely chopped

Preheat the oven to 200°C/Fan 180°C Fan/Gas 6.

For the meatballs, heat the oil in a frying pan and cook the onion until soft and translucent. Add the garlic and cook for a further minute. Remove the pan from the heat and leave to cool.

Put the cooled onion and garlic in a bowl, add the rest of the meatball ingredients and mix thoroughly with your hands. Shape the mixture into balls between the size of a walnut and a golf ball – each roughly 40g in weight. You should have about 24 meatballs. Put the balls on a baking tray and bake them for 12–15 minutes until cooked through.

To make the gravy, melt the butter in a saucepan that's large enough to hold the meatballs. Add the flour, stir it into the butter, then cook for 5–10 minutes, stirring until the mixture is golden-brown. Add the white wine and stir vigorously until well incorporated. Gradually add the beef stock, stirring well in between each addition to avoid lumps, until you have a slightly thickened gravy. Add the cream and the jam, and mix to combine. Season with salt and pepper.

Remove the meatballs from the oven and place them in the pan of gravy. Simmer gently for 5–10 minutes to allow the flavours to combine. Serve with a sprinkling of dill, more jam on the side and lots of mashed potato.

Mince and herby dumplings

What's not to love about mince and dumplings? This is a total northern classic that we've both eaten since we were kids and still love. When it comes to the dumplings, though, our tastes differ. Dave prefers a natural dumpling – just steamed like this – while Kingy likes his slightly tanned. If you're with Si, just pop the dish under the grill to brown your dumplings and give them a crunchy crust.

Serves 6

2 tbsp vegetable oil

1 large onion, thinly sliced

2 garlic cloves, finely chopped

2 celery sticks, finely sliced

2 carrots, diced

500g beef mince

400g can of chopped tomatoes

2 tbsp tomato purée

450ml beef stock

pinch of caster sugar

1 bay leaf

sea salt and black pepper

Dumplings

250g self-raising flour

125g beef suet, shredded

½ tsp fine sea salt

2 tbsp finely chopped fresh parsley

1 tsp finely chopped rosemary

1 tsp finely chopped thyme

For the mince, heat the oil in a large pan and cook the onion, garlic, celery and carrots for 15 minutes. Stir occasionally until the veg are softened and lightly coloured. Add the beef and cook for a further 5 minutes until the mince begins to brown, stirring regularly to break up the meat.

Add the tomatoes, tomato purée, beef stock, sugar and bay leaf. Season with salt and black pepper, then bring to the boil. Reduce the heat and simmer the mince gently for 20 minutes, stirring occasionally.

To make the dumplings, put the flour in a bowl and stir in the suet, salt and herbs. Make a well in the centre and add enough cold water to make a soft, spongy dough – you'll need about 200ml. Lightly flour your hands and roll the mixture into 12 small balls.

Stir the mince well and remove the pan from the heat. Drop the dumplings on top of the mince, then cover with a tightly fitting lid and return the pan to a medium heat. Cook for 18–20 minutes or until the dumplings are well risen. Serve with some green vegetables.

Hand-rolled spinach pasta with paprika meatballs

Pasta has become a staple in British kitchens and while we have a way to go to catch up with the Italians, we're eating loads. This is our version of 'pici' pasta, which is rolled out to the thickness of a pencil and looks like fat spaghetti – the kids will enjoy helping to make it. Delicious with these meatballs.

Serves 4

————

Pasta

200g spinach, well washed
300–350g Italian '00' flour
  (strong white flour)

Meatballs

1 tbsp olive oil, plus extra
1 onion, finely chopped
2 garlic cloves, chopped
300g minced beef
300g minced pork
100g white breadcrumbs
50ml soured cream
  or crème fraiche
2 tsp sweet
  smoked paprika
1 tsp hot smoked paprika
1 tsp dried oregano
2 tbsp chopped parsley
1 egg
sea salt and black pepper

Roast tomatoes

400g cherry tomatoes,
  halved
leaves from 1 thyme sprig
2 garlic cloves, finely sliced
2–3 tbsp olive oil

To garnish

fresh basil leaves
Parmesan shavings

To make the pasta, shake off any excess water from the spinach and put it in a food processor with 300g of the flour. Blend until the spinach has completely broken down and formed a dough with the flour. Check the dough – if it is very sticky, add more flour. The texture should be soft and very slightly tacky.

To roll out the pasta, pull off small balls, about the size of a large marble. Roll these between your hands, then lay them out on a work surface and roll them lightly with both hands, moving from the centre outwards, to make long pencil-shaped pieces. If the dough is very sticky, dust your hands with a little flour, but try not to use too much as it makes the pasta much harder to roll. The pasta can be cooked right away, in a large pan of boiling, salted water, or it can be dried out. If you are cooking from fresh, it will take 5 minutes; if it is dry, it will take 8–10 minutes.

For the meatballs, heat the oil in a frying pan and add the onion. Cook over a medium to low heat until very soft and translucent, then add the garlic and continue to cook for another minute or so. Remove from the heat and cool.

Put the beef and pork in a bowl with the breadcrumbs, soured cream or crème fraiche, both paprikas, the herbs and egg. Add the onion and garlic and season very generously. Mix thoroughly. Take a small amount of the mixture and fry it, then taste for seasoning and adjust accordingly – meatball mixture often needs more salt than you think. Form the mixture into 20 balls.

You can bake or fry the meatballs. To bake, preheat the oven to 200°C/Fan 180°C Fan/Gas 6. Place the meatballs on a baking sheet and cook them for 18–20 minutes until well browned and piping hot in the centre, turning them halfway through. Or, heat some oil in a large frying pan and fry the meatballs in batches, turning them regularly.

For the roast tomatoes, lay the tomatoes in a roasting tin, cut-side up, and sprinkle with salt, thyme leaves, garlic and the oil. Roast for about 10 minutes, or until well softened and very slightly browned round the edges. Spoon the meatballs and tomatoes with all the pan juices over the pasta and serve with plenty of basil and Parmesan shavings.

Easy Biker lasagne

Lasagne has become a British classic. It's on nearly every pub menu and it's certainly a favourite of ours. We've even been known to enjoy it with chips! Over the years we've made lasagne with meatballs, fish, everything but the kitchen sink, but now we've gone back to basics. This new recipe has a simple meat sauce and no need to make a béchamel – we use plenty of ricotta cheese instead. If you're cooking for two, you could make the full amount of sauce and stash some in the freezer for another time. Then just halve the rest of the ingredients.

Serves 4–6

Meat sauce

2 tbsp olive oil

2 onions, finely chopped

3 celery sticks, finely chopped

2 carrots, finely chopped

3 garlic cloves, finely chopped

750g minced beef

250ml red wine

600g canned tomatoes

1 tbsp ground oregano

2 bay leaves

sea salt and black pepper

To assemble

9 dried lasagne sheets

300g ricotta

400g mozzarella

100g Parmesan, grated

bunch of basil, shredded, a few whole reserved for the top

First make the meat sauce. Heat a tablespoon of the oil in a large pan and add the onions, celery and carrots. Cook over a gentle heat until the onions are translucent and soft, then add the garlic and cook for a further 3–4 minutes.

Add the remaining oil to a large frying pan. Fry the beef, leaving it until a brown crust has developed on the underside before breaking it up and turning it over. It's best to do this in a few batches – if you crowd the pan the meat will stew in its own juices instead of searing.

Add the beef to the vegetables, then turn the heat up high and add the red wine. Boil until the wine is reduced by at least half, then add the tomatoes and herbs. Season with salt and pepper. Bring back to the boil, then turn down the heat, cover and simmer for an hour. Remove the lid and continue to simmer, stirring regularly, until the sauce has reduced down – this will probably take another 15 minutes.

Preheat the oven to 200°C/Fan 180°C/Gas 6. To assemble the lasagne, spread a third of the meat sauce in the base of a rectangular ovenproof dish, large enough for 3 sheets of lasagne. Cover with lasagne sheets and then add another third of the meat sauce. Spoon 100g of the ricotta in teaspoons over the sauce. Add 100g of the mozzarella and a few basil leaves.

Add another layer of pasta and repeat with the same quantities of meat sauce and cheeses. Top with a final layer of pasta, the remaining meat sauce, mozzarella and ricotta, then sprinkle the Parmesan on top.

Bake in the oven for 45–50 minutes until the pasta is cooked through and the top is a rich dark brown and bubbling. Remove the lasagne from the oven and leave it to stand for at least 10 minutes before cutting.

COSY
COMFORT
CLASSICS

Biker breakfast pizza

Normally we're quite purist about our pizzas but then we got the idea of combining the classic full English with our Italian favourite. It's a fab hangover cure and guess what? You don't need toast! The thing to do if you want to have this for breakfast is to make the dough the night before so it can rise slowly overnight in the fridge.

Makes 2 large pizzas

———

Pizza dough

300g strong white flour, plus extra for dusting

7g instant yeast

1 tsp salt

2 tbsp olive oil

175ml tepid water

Tomato sauce

200g tomato passata

1 tbsp tomato paste

2 garlic cloves

1 tsp dried oregano

handful of fresh basil leaves

sea salt and black pepper

Topping (enough for 2 pizzas)

4 fat sausages, peeled and broken up into small pieces

8 rashers of bacon, cut into pieces

4 slices of black pudding, broken up (optional)

4 field mushrooms, thinly sliced

4 medium tomatoes, sliced

2–4 eggs

2 mozzarella balls, broken up

olive oil, for drizzling

To make the pizza dough, put the flour in a large bowl and sprinkle in the yeast. Stir thoroughly before adding the salt. Mix the olive oil with the water, then make a well in the centre of the flour and start pouring in the liquid. Stir until you have a fairly wet dough, then turn it out and knead until it is no longer sticky, but soft and pliable.

Put the dough in a bowl, cover and leave it to rise for an hour – or overnight in the fridge. Knock it back and divide it into 2 large pieces.

When you are ready to cook the pizzas, preheat the oven to its highest setting and heat 2 baking trays or pizza stones. Shape the pizzas into large circles, then dust 2 more baking trays with flour and put the pizza bases on them – this is so you can slide them straight on to the hot baking trays or pizza stones in the oven.

Make the tomato sauce by blending all the sauce ingredients together in a food processor with plenty of salt and pepper.

Spread a small amount of the tomato sauce over the pizza bases, then top with the pieces of sausage, bacon, black pudding, if using, mushrooms and tomatoes.

Break one or more eggs on top of each pizza, making sure that the eggs are contained by other ingredients so that the white doesn't run off – you can turn up the edges of the pizza base slightly to make sure. Sprinkle with mozzarella, then drizzle with olive oil.

Bake in the oven for 8–10 minutes, or until the pizzas are lovely and crisp and the toppings are cooked.

Hairy Biker tip: We've used a really quick, no-cook tomato sauce here for speed, but you could make a regular sauce if you like. And if you prefer, you could make 4 smaller pizzas.

Thai vegetable curry

Whether you're in Bangkok or Brum, a Thai curry makes a great supper. These beautifully flavoursome curries are hugely popular in the UK now and have become regular items on many menus. Our version does have lots of ingredients but once you've prepped them it's really just an assembly job.

Serves 4

2 tbsp vegetable oil

1 large leek, thinly sliced

2 garlic cloves, crushed
to a paste

1 large red chilli, trimmed
and finely chopped

2 tbsp Thai red curry
paste (shop-bought or
see page 275)

4 fresh lime leaves

2 carrots, roughly chopped

400g can of chopped
tomatoes

400g can of coconut milk

250ml vegetable stock

1 small cauliflower,
trimmed and cut
into florets

½ small butternut
squash, flesh cut into
2.5cm chunks

175g snake or French
beans, trimmed

225g can of bamboo
shoots, drained

bunch of fresh coriander,
chopped

handful of fresh bean
sprouts, to garnish

Heat a tablespoon of the oil in a large wok over a high heat. When the oil is smoking, add the leek, garlic and chilli and stir-fry for 3–5 minutes, or until softened but not browned. Add the 2 tablespoons of curry paste and fry for 2–3 minutes, stirring well.

Add the lime leaves, carrots and chopped tomatoes, then stir in the coconut milk and vegetable stock. Bring the mixture to the boil, then reduce the heat and simmer, uncovered, for 10 minutes.

Add the cauliflower florets, squash, beans and bamboo shoots and continue to simmer for 12–15 minutes, or until the squash is tender and the sauce has thickened slightly and reduced in volume. Stir in the chopped coriander.

Serve with rice and garnish with a few bean sprouts.

Salmon pie with spinach

Not many people know this about us but we are both keen fishermen. One time when we'd caught loads of trout in a river in Scotland we made this pie and it was so good, we wanted you to have some too. We found it tastes even better with salmon which is harder to catch but easy to find in the supermarket!

Serves 4

4–5 tbsp hollandaise
    sauce (see page 274)
500g salmon fillet
450–500g baby leaf
    spinach
375–500g pre-rolled
    puff pastry
grated zest of 1 lemon
1 tbsp finely chopped
    tarragon (optional)
1 egg, lightly beaten
sea salt and black pepper

First make the hollandaise sauce (see page 274). Leave it to cool by putting the bowl of sauce into a larger bowl filled with iced water.

For the pie, put the salmon in a large pan and add cold water just to cover. Bring to the boil, then cover the pan and simmer the fish for 2 minutes. Remove the pan from the heat and leave for a further 5 minutes. Strain off the liquid and leave the salmon to cool. When it has cooled, flake the flesh, keeping the pieces as large as possible.

Wash the spinach, then without draining it too thoroughly, put it in a pan. Place the pan over a medium heat and push the spinach down with a wooden spoon – it will wilt down quite quickly. When it has completely collapsed leave to cool, then squeeze out as much liquid as possible.

Preheat the oven to 200°C/Fan180°C/Gas 6. Unroll the puff pastry. Arrange half of the salmon over the bottom half of the pastry, leaving a 2cm border along the bottom. Season with salt and pepper, and top with half the spinach.

Stir the lemon zest and the tarragon, if using, into the hollandaise, then spread half of the hollandaise over the spinach. Repeat these layers with the remaining salmon, spinach and hollandaise.

Brush the border and exposed pastry with beaten egg. Fold the pastry over and roll the edges to seal. Brush the pie with beaten egg and cut a few slits along the top of the pastry.

Bake the pie in the oven for 35–45 minutes, or until the pastry has puffed up and is a rich golden-brown, and the filling is piping hot.

Beer-battered scampi with tartare sauce

Proper North Sea scampi, AKA Dublin Bay prawns or langoustine tails, are the best in the world and we love 'em. We cooked this fantastic scampi dish with a super-light, crispy batter on our 'Best of British' series and it disappeared faster than Ronnie Biggs! The crew loved it and that's always a good sign. Great with the home-made tartare sauce too.

Serves 4

vegetable oil

4 tbsp plain flour

½ tsp fine sea salt

16–20 scampi tails, peeled and thawed (if frozen)

lemon wedges, to serve

Batter

30g cornflour

100g plain flour

½ tsp fine sea salt

160ml real ale

1 tbsp white wine vinegar

Tartare sauce

1 egg yolk

½ tbsp white wine vinegar

1 tsp Dijon mustard

pinch of caster sugar

pinch of fine sea salt

75ml vegetable oil

25ml extra virgin olive oil

25g capers, drained and roughly chopped

25g cornichons, drained and thinly sliced

1 tbsp chopped parsley

1 tbsp chopped tarragon

black pepper

First make the tartare sauce. Using a balloon whisk, whisk the egg yolk, vinegar, mustard, sugar and salt in a bowl until well combined. Gradually add the oils, a few drops at a time, and keep whisking until the sauce is smooth and very thick. Stir in the capers, cornichons, parsley, tarragon and plenty of black pepper. Cover the surface of the sauce with cling film and set it aside for 20 minutes.

Mix the cornflour, plain flour and salt together in a large bowl to make the batter. Make a well in the centre and stir in two-thirds of the ale, then whisk to make a smooth batter. Gently whisk in the remaining ale and the vinegar. Set aside.

Fill a large pan or a deep-fat fryer two-thirds full with vegetable oil. Heat the oil to 190°C. Use a thermometer to check the temperature if you're not using a deep-fat fryer and be careful – hot oil is dangerous so don't leave it unattended.

Put the 4 tablespoons of flour in a plastic or paper bag and season with salt. Add the scampi tails, one at a time, and shake to coat them in the seasoned flour.

Stir the batter and, using tongs, dip a piece of floured scampi into the batter until thoroughly coated. Gently place the scampi in the hot oil. Quickly repeat with 3 or 4 more pieces, adding them to the pan, and cook them for 3–4 minutes until they're golden-brown and crisp.

Remove the scampi, drain them on kitchen paper and keep them warm. Bring the oil back to 190°C, and cook the remaining scampi in 2 or 3 more batches.

Serve the scampi with the tartare sauce and lemon wedges.

Really good kedgeree

We've called this really good kedgeree because it is! All too often kedgeree can be dry and have the odour of a kipper's breath, but done properly this is an Anglo-Indian/Hairy Biker masterpiece. We know it was a traditional country house breakfast in Downton Abbey days, but we think it makes a great supper dish too.

Serves 6

475g undyed smoked
    haddock fillet, halved

2 bay leaves

200g basmati rice,
    rinsed in cold water
    and drained

4 eggs

100g frozen peas (optional)

40g butter

1 tbsp vegetable oil

1 onion, finely chopped

1 heaped tbsp
    medium curry powder

3 tbsp double cream

3 tbsp chopped
    fresh parsley

juice of ½ lemon

black pepper

Place the haddock in a large frying pan, skin-side up. Pour over 500ml of water, add the bay leaves and bring the water to a gentle simmer. Cook the fish for 8–10 minutes until it is just done and flakes easily. Drain it in a colander set over a bowl, reserve the cooking liquor and discard the bay leaves.

Pour the cooking liquor into a pan and stir in the rice. Cover the pan with a lid and bring the liquor to the boil, then reduce the heat and simmer very gently for 10 minutes. Turn off the heat and leave the rice covered for 3–5 minutes longer. By this time it should have absorbed all the liquid.

While the rice is cooking, bring some water to the boil in another pan, add the eggs and cook them for 8 minutes. Drain them in a sieve and cool under cold running water, then peel them and set aside. Cook the peas, if using, in a small pan of boiling water and drain.

Melt the butter with the oil in a large pan and cook the onion over a low heat for 5 minutes until softened, stirring occasionally. Add the curry powder and cook for another 3 minutes, stirring constantly. Add the cooked rice to the pan and stir in the onion. Then add the peas, cream, parsley and a few twists of black pepper.

Flake the fish into chunky pieces and add them to the pan. Gently stir in the lemon juice and cook for a couple of minutes. Cut the eggs into quarters and place them on the rice. Cover the pan with a lid and heat through for 2–3 minutes or until the eggs are warm, then serve.

Hairy Biker tip: If not serving immediately, tip the kedgeree into a warm dish and dot with a few cubes of butter. Cover the dish with foil and keep warm in a low oven for up to 20 minutes before serving.

Bengali fish curry

We're well known for our love of curry, which has become as much a part of British cuisine as egg and chips, and this is one of our favourites. We first ate this on our 'Hairy Bikers' Cook Off' show when it was made by one of the competing families, who were first generation British-Bengali. It was so good we've been making it ever since and we've found that a combination of mustard seeds and English mustard powder brings just the right level of heat and flavour. Don't reduce the amount of oil in the recipe as you need it to help thicken the sauce.

Serves 2

————

2 sea bass or sea bream fillets (each about 200g), scales removed but skin on

1 tsp sea salt flakes, plus extra to season

¼ tsp cayenne pepper

2½ tsp English mustard powder

4 tbsp vegetable oil

1 heaped tsp yellow mustard seeds

¾ tsp black mustard seeds

¾ tsp cumin seeds

1 onion, finely sliced

2 long green chillies, halved but not seeded

1 bay leaf

½ tsp ground turmeric

½ tsp garam masala

150g ripe tomatoes, roughly chopped

black pepper

Cut the fish fillets into strips about 7cm wide. Put them in a bowl and toss with the salt, cayenne pepper, half a teaspoon of the mustard powder and lots of black pepper.

Mix the remaining mustard powder with 300ml of water, adding it gradually and stirring constantly until you have thin yellow liquid. Set aside.

Heat the oil in a large frying pan and fry a batch of the fish, skin-side down, over a high heat for a minute, or until the skin begins to crisp – don't overcrowd the pan. Turn the fillets over and cook on the other side for a further minute. Remove the fish and set it aside on a plate while you cook the rest.

Once all the fish is cooked, put the pan back on the heat and add the mustard seeds and cumin seeds. Cook for a few seconds, stirring constantly. Add the onion, chillies and bay leaf and cook for about 5 minutes, stirring, until the onion is softened and pale golden-brown. Sprinkle over the turmeric and garam masala, add the chopped tomatoes and cook for 2 minutes more, stirring constantly.

Stir in the reserved mustard liquid and bring to a simmer. Cook for a few minutes, or until the sauce has thickened and the volume of liquid has reduced by about one-third. The spices should have mellowed and the sauce should coat the back of a spoon. Return the fish to the pan and warm through in the bubbling sauce for 2 minutes until hot. Serve immediately with rice.

Seafood chowder

A chowder is a thick hearty soup, containing shellfish or other seafood. The term is generally thought to have started in the US, but in 16th century Cornwall fish sellers were called 'jowters' so it is possible that chowders started way back then. Whatever its origins, chowder is a favourite of ours and certainly deserves classic status. When we did our 'Food Tour' series we made a cockle chowder on the beach in Southend. It was great but not everyone is a fan of cockles so we've come up with an easy version using a pack of frozen seafood mix. What could be simpler? And it's a cracking good dish too.

Serves 4

25g butter

50g streaky bacon, cut into small strips

1 onion, diced

2 leeks, cut into rounds

2 celery sticks, sliced

1 tbsp plain flour (optional)

100ml white wine

300ml milk

300ml fish or chicken stock

300g floury potatoes, diced

2 bay leaves

2 thyme sprigs

1 mace blade

100ml double cream

500g frozen seafood mix, defrosted and well drained

2 tbsp finely chopped parsley, to serve

sea salt and black pepper

Heat the butter in a large pan. Add the bacon, onion, leeks and celery and cook over a low heat for several minutes until the vegetables have started to soften and the bacon has rendered out some its fat and started to crisp up.

The potatoes should thicken the chowder nicely, but you can also add flour to thicken if you want. If using the flour, stir it into the buttery vegetables, then pour in the white wine. Allow the wine to bubble up, then stir until you have a thick paste. Add the milk and stock at the same time, along with the potatoes, herbs and mace, then season with salt and pepper. Bring the liquid almost to the boil, stirring constantly, then turn down the heat to a gentle simmer. Continue to cook, stirring regularly, until the vegetables are very tender and the soup has thickened.

Add the cream to the soup and cook for 2–3 minutes until piping hot. Add all the seafood and continue to cook for a further 3 minutes, then check the seasoning and add more salt and pepper if necessary. Serve the chowder in bowls and garnish with chopped parsley.

Classic chicken cobbler

A cobbler topping is like a cross between scones and dumplings and definitely not a load of old cobblers! The trick is to have the sumptuous stew oozing up between the chinks in the cobbles so they are soggy on the bottom but crispy on top – a perfect combo. We first ate cobblers in the US, but we've come up with a few of our own versions since then and now they're just as popular in Britain.

Serves 6

1 tbsp olive oil

15g butter

4 leeks, cut into 2–3cm rounds

4 skinless, boneless chicken thigh fillets and 2 breasts (about 800g), cut into bite-sized pieces

2 garlic cloves, finely chopped

2 large tarragon sprigs, finely chopped

100ml white wine

150g ham (optional), chopped

1 egg, beaten

Sauce

50g butter

50g flour

400ml chicken stock

1 tsp Dijon mustard (optional)

50ml double cream

sea salt and black pepper

Topping

250g plain flour

2 tsp baking powder

1 egg

100ml buttermilk

Heat the olive oil and butter in a large frying pan that has a lid. Add the leeks and cook gently for about 5 minutes, until they are starting to soften, then add the chicken, garlic and tarragon. Stir for a minute so that everything is covered in the buttery juices, then pour in the wine. Bring to the boil, then turn down the heat and cover the pan. Leave to poach gently for about 10 minutes.

Meanwhile, start to make the sauce. Melt the butter in a pan, then stir in the flour until combined. Continue to stir for 3–4 minutes to make sure the flour is nicely toasted. Start adding the chicken stock a little at the time, stirring in between each addition until the sauce is completely smooth. Season with salt and pepper and set aside.

Using a slotted spoon, transfer the chicken and leeks to a large casserole dish or pie dish and stir in the ham, if using. Add any liquid from the frying pan to the sauce, along with the mustard, if using, and the cream. Pour this over the chicken and leeks.

Preheat the oven to 200°C/Fan 180°C/Gas 6. For the cobbler topping, put the flour and baking powder into a bowl and season generously with salt. Whisk the egg and buttermilk together, then combine with the dry ingredients. The dough should come together into a firm, slightly sticky ball. Divide the dough into 8–9 balls. Flatten these out slightly and arrange them over the chicken.

Brush the cobbler with beaten egg and put the dish in the oven. Bake for 25–30 minutes until the topping is well risen and golden-brown and the filling is piping hot.

Chicken and pumpkin curry

We Brits are good at bringing home the best flavours from around the world. Curries of all kinds are British classics these days and Caribbean curries like this one certainly have their place. It is worth looking for Caribbean curry powder as its unique flavour adds so much to this dish. We can't guarantee this dish will make you run as fast as Usain Bolt but it will make you smile when you taste it.

Serves 4

8 bone-in chicken thighs
juice of 1 lime
sea salt and black pepper

Marinade
4 spring onions, chopped
4 garlic cloves, chopped
20g fresh root ginger,
    peeled and chopped
2 scotch bonnets, seeded
    and finely chopped
zest and juice of 1 lime
2 tbsp medium curry
    blend, preferably
    Caribbean
½ tsp ground allspice

Curry
1 tbsp vegetable oil
1 onion, thickly sliced
300ml chicken stock
2 tomatoes, peeled
    and diced
2 large thyme sprigs
2 bay leaves
400g pumpkin, cut
    into large chunks
juice of ½ a lime
1 tsp rum (optional)

To serve
sliced spring onions
chopped parsley
    or coriander

Skin the chicken thighs, put them in a bowl and season them with salt and pepper. Put all the marinade ingredients into a small food processor and blend to a paste – add a little water if needed.

Pour the marinade over the chicken and mix thoroughly to make sure the chicken is completely covered. Cover and leave for as long as you can – at least a couple of hours, but overnight is better. If you are leaving the chicken for longer than an hour, put it in the fridge.

For the curry, heat the vegetable oil in a large flameproof casserole dish. Add the onion and cook it over a medium heat for several minutes until it starts to turn golden-brown. Add the chicken and the marinade to the dish – the idea is not to brown the chicken but to cook the marinade ingredients for a couple of minutes. Add the stock (or water is fine if you don't have any stock).

Add the tomatoes, thyme and bay leaves and season with salt and pepper. Bring to the boil, then turn the heat down, cover, and leave to simmer for about 40 minutes.

Add the pumpkin and cook for a further 10 minutes, covered. Pour in the lime juice and the rum, if using. Remove the lid and cook for another 5–10 minutes to reduce the sauce slightly and finish off cooking the pumpkin.

Serve topped with sliced spring onions and fresh parsley or coriander. Some steamed rice is a perfect accompaniment.

Hairy Biker tips: If you'd like your curry more coconutty, add some grated coconut cream at the end or 100ml of coconut milk with the stock.

And if you want a bit less heat, just use one scotch bonnet.

Chicken tikka masala

Once voted Britain's favourite curry, this dish might actually have been invented in Britain by mixing proper Indian chicken tikka with a curry sauce to satisfy our love of gravy. As well as having fab flavour, this is a great prepare-ahead dish – the chicken can be marinated ahead of time and the sauce can be made and stored, as it is only after the chicken has been grilled that it is added to the sauce. If you don't have any Kashmiri chilli powder, you could use two tablespoons of sweet paprika mixed with a teaspoon of medium chilli powder.

Serves 4

Spice mix

2 tbsp ground cumin

2 tbsp ground coriander

2 tbsp Kashmiri chilli powder

1 tsp ground turmeric

½ tsp ground cinnamon

½ tsp ground fenugreek

pinch of cloves

Chicken tikka

1 tbsp spice mix or 1 tbsp tandoori masala powder

3 garlic cloves, crushed

20g fresh root ginger, grated

2 tbsp yoghurt

juice of ½ lemon

4 boneless chicken breasts, skinned and diced

fresh coriander, to serve

Sauce

3 tbsp vegetable oil

2 onions, finely sliced

4 garlic cloves, crushed

25g fresh root ginger, grated or finely chopped

1 tbsp spice mix

3 tbsp tomato purée

½ tsp caster sugar

2 tbsp yoghurt

If making the spice mix from scratch, simply mix the ground spices together until they are completely combined into a rich ochre mixture.

Next marinade the chicken. Combine the spice mix with the garlic, ginger and yoghurt. Put the chicken in a bowl and season it well with salt. Add the lemon juice and toss the chicken pieces in it so it is well coated, then pour over the spice and yoghurt mix. Mix thoroughly, then cover and put it in the fridge for several hours, or preferably overnight.

Next make the sauce. Heat the oil in a pan and add the onions, garlic and ginger. Cover and cook over a medium-low heat for 10 minutes, stirring regularly until the onion has softened. Remove the lid and cook for a further 5 minutes over a slightly higher heat to allow the onions to take on some colour.

Add the spices and stir for another minute or so, then add the tomato purée and sugar. Season with salt and pepper, then stir for a few minutes. Add 400ml of water and bring to the boil. Turn down the heat and simmer gently for a further 5 minutes.

Blitz the contents of the saucepan with either a stick blender or by transferring the mixture to a jug blender. The sauce should be completely smooth. Stir in the yoghurt. If using the sauce straight away, keep it warm while you cook the chicken. Otherwise it can be stored in the fridge for several days until you need it.

To cook the chicken, heat a griddle until it is too hot to hold your hand over. Remove t he chicken from the marinade, wiping off any excess, then place it on the griddle. Cook for several minutes or until char lines appear and the pieces lift off the griddle easily. Cook them on the other side until just cooked through. You may have to do this in a couple of batches. Alternatively, heat up your grill to its highest setting and grill the chicken for 4–5 minutes on each side.

Transfer the chicken to the sauce and simmer until everything is piping hot. Serve sprinkled with coriander and with lemon wedges for squeezing over.

Spicy sausage pasta

We all love our pasta and it's become a favourite quick midweek supper in many households, including ours. Spanish chorizo is a British favourite too, so we've combined a bit of Spain and a bit of Italy in this easy recipe. It's important to use fresh tomatoes, as they make the sauce sweet and creamy, not acidic. Using a little of the cooking water in the sauce is a great trick we've picked up. The starch in the water helps to thicken the sauce.

Serves 4

150g soft cooking chorizo, skinned and finely chopped

1 onion, finely chopped

1 red pepper, finely diced

3 medium, very ripe tomatoes, skinned and finely chopped

small bunch of parsley, finely chopped

400g linguine

sea salt and black pepper

Put a large frying pan over a medium-low heat. Add the chorizo and fry it gently, squashing it down with the back of a wooden spoon. The idea is to break it up as much as possible. When the chorizo is lightly coloured and has rendered out most of its fat, remove it from the pan with a slotted spoon and put it on some kitchen paper to drain. Leave the chorizo oil in the pan.

Add the onion and red pepper to the pan. Cook them over a gentle heat in the chorizo oil until very soft and translucent. Add the tomatoes and half the parsley and season with salt and pepper. Continue to cook until the tomatoes have completely broken down and reduced.

While the sauce is cooking, bring a large saucepan of water to the boil. Add plenty of salt, then cook the pasta until just done but still with a little bite to it. Reserve a ladle or so of the cooking water, then drain.

Add about 100ml of the cooking water to the sauce and simmer for another minute or so until very slightly reduced until it is no longer runny. Toss with the pasta and serve immediately with the remaining parsley sprinkled over.

Lancashire hotpot

A hotpot is too good to be kept captive in Lancashire. This recipe is an old favourite of ours and a true-blue classic so we just had to include it in this book. If you don't like kidneys leave them out, but the black pudding does add richness and flavour so we recommend it. The beauty of a hotpot is that the lower layers of potatoes are gloriously soft and gooey, as they are cooked in the meat juices, while those on the top are super-crispy.

Serves 6

2 tbsp olive oil

1kg neck of lamb, chopped into bite-sized pieces

4 lambs' kidneys, cleaned, trimmed, cut into quarters

2 onions, sliced

½ tsp salt, plus extra to season

1 tbsp plain flour

250ml lamb stock

1 thyme sprig

2 fresh bay leaves

1 tbsp Worcestershire sauce

50g butter, cut into cubes, plus extra for greasing

1kg potatoes, sliced

2 x 250g black pudding rings, outer casing removed, thickly sliced

sea salt and black pepper

Preheat the oven to 180°C/Fan 160°C/Gas 4.

Heat the olive oil in a pan and fry the lamb and kidneys for a minute or so on both sides, or until golden-brown all over. Remove them from the pan and set aside.

Add the onions and salt to the pan and cook for 2–3 minutes, or until the onions have softened. Stir in the flour until the onions are well coated with the flour.

Add the stock to the pan along with the thyme, bay leaves and Worcestershire sauce. Stir and simmer for 8–10 minutes, or until thickened slightly.

Take a flameproof casserole dish that has a lid and butter the inside. Place a layer of potatoes (about a third) over the bottom of the dish and season with salt and pepper.

Spoon in half of the browned lamb and lambs' kidneys, then lay over half the black pudding slices and pour over half the thickened stock mixture. Repeat the layering process until all the potatoes, lamb and kidneys, black pudding and stock have been used, finishing with a layer of potatoes on top. Dot the potatoes with the butter, then cover the dish with a lid.

Place the casserole dish in the oven and cook for 25 minutes, then remove the lid and cook for a further 20 minutes, or until the potatoes are golden-brown on top. Serve with some green veg and enjoy!

Liver and bacon with onions and gravy

We cooked this often overlooked classic in the big top on our 'Mums Know Best' show and it went down a storm. Loads of our guests told us how they had forgotten just how great this wholesome British dish could be. The secret is to cook the liver carefully – and not overcook it until it is leathery like we all remember from school dinners. The gravy just begs to be poured over some buttery mash (see page 266).

Serves 4

450g lambs' liver, sliced

25g butter

1 tbsp vegetable oil

2 tbsp plain flour

125g streaky bacon
  rashers, rinds removed

1 onion, sliced

500ml beef stock

1–2 tsp tomato ketchup

sea salt and black pepper

Rinse the lambs' liver in a colander under cold water. Drain it well on kitchen paper and pat it dry. Melt half the butter with the oil in a large frying pan over a high heat.

Put the flour in a large bowl and season it with plenty of salt and pepper. Add half the lambs' liver and toss it lightly in the flour to coat it. Place each slice carefully in the hot fat and cook for a minute or so on each side until lightly browned but not completely cooked through. Transfer to a plate. Toss the remaining liver in the seasoned flour and brown as before, then transfer to the plate.

Cut each bacon rasher into 4 or 5 pieces. Reduce the heat and melt the remaining butter in the pan. Add the onion and cook for a minute or so, while stirring. Add the bacon and cook with the onion for 8–10 minutes or until the onion is pale golden-brown and the bacon is beginning to crisp, stirring often.

Sprinkle the rest of the flour into the pan and stir it into the onion and bacon for a minute or so. Add the stock, bring to a simmer and cook over a medium heat until the gravy is thickened. Add a dash of tomato ketchup and season with salt and pepper.

Put the liver back in the pan and warm it through in the onion gravy for a minute or so until hot. Serve the liver and bacon with some lovely mash (see page 266) and greens.

Sausage and ale casserole

This cracking casserole made with good British bangers and ale was inspired by the stews made with beer that we enjoyed on one of our very early road trips to Belgium. The gravy is to die for and, as British sausages have got better and better over the years, we think this is a recipe that more than deserves classic status. A big pile of buttery mash is a must with this one.

Serves 4–6

———

1 tbsp vegetable oil

12 good-quality pork sausages

2 medium onions, chopped

2 celery sticks, trimmed and thinly sliced

3 carrots, thickly sliced

500ml India pale ale

150ml beef stock

2 tbsp tomato purée

2 tbsp light muscovado sugar

1 bay leaf

splash of Worcestershire sauce

2 medium leeks, trimmed and cut into 2cm slices

1 tbsp cornflour

1 tsp flaked sea salt, plus extra to season

chopped parsley, to garnish

black pepper

Heat the oil in a large frying pan and fry the sausages over a medium heat for 8–10 minutes. Turn them regularly until they're nicely browned all over. Transfer the sausages to a large flameproof casserole dish.

Add the onions, celery and carrots to the frying pan – there should be enough fat from the sausages but add an extra splash of oil if you need to. Cook the veg over a medium-high heat, stirring regularly, for 5 minutes or until they are beginning to soften and lightly colour. Tip the vegetables into the dish with the sausages.

Pour the ale and stock into the casserole dish. Stir in the tomato purée, sugar, bay leaf and a splash of Worcestershire sauce. Bring to the boil, then reduce the heat, cover the dish with a lid and leave to simmer gently for 30 minutes, stirring occasionally.

Add the leeks to the casserole dish and simmer uncovered for 5 minutes, stirring occasionally. Mix the cornflour with a tablespoon of cold water until smooth. Stir this into the casserole and cook for another 2–3 minutes, stirring regularly until the sauce has thickened.

Remove the pan from the heat, season with salt and pepper and sprinkle with chopped parsley before serving with mashed potatoes (see page 266).

Jerk pork chops

We're a nation of spice lovers – and not just curry. Thanks to our West Indian community, jerk dishes have become as popular in Britain as in the Caribbean and have a well-established place in our menus. They're just the thing for a barbecue and dead simple to make – the marinade does all the work and you can use it on other meat too, not just pork. The jerk seasoning is quite hot but you can use less chilli if you don't like things hot, hot, hot. Serve this with rice and peas (see page 270) for the true Caribbean vibe.

Serves 4

———

4 large pork chops
  (preferably fatty and
  on the bone)

1 tsp salt

Jerk marinade

bunch of spring onions,
  roughly chopped

1–2 scotch bonnet chillies,
  seeded, depending on
  how hot you want it

6 garlic cloves

30g fresh root
  ginger, chopped

leaves from a large t
  hyme sprig

2 tbsp red wine vinegar

2 tbsp vegetable oil

2 tbsp soft dark brown
  sugar

1 tbsp allspice berries,
  crushed

1 tsp cinnamon

1 tsp smoked paprika

good grating of nutmeg

1 tsp black pepper

To make the marinade, put all the ingredients into a food processor or blender and blitz until you have a fairly liquid paste. Put the pork chops in a bowl and season them with the teaspoon of salt, then pour over the marinade. Cover and leave for at least a couple of hours, preferably overnight.

When you are ready to cook the chops, heat your grill to medium-high or get your barbecue going. Grill the chops for 3–4 minutes on each side, depending on thickness, then leave them to rest for a few minutes.

SMASHING SUNDAY DINNERS

Chestnut and mushroom pie

We love a pie and what's more British than a chestnut? We cooked this on our 'Comfort Food' series but we weren't quite happy with the recipe. We wanted to make something that would be a really lovely vegetarian Sunday lunch. We've had another go for this book and now we think we've come up with something fab-u-lous!

Serves 6

———

50g butter

1 onion, finely chopped

600g mixture of fresh
  mushrooms, sliced

3 garlic cloves, chopped

large thyme sprig,
  leaves only

1 tsp dried sage

30g plain flour

100ml white wine

300ml mushroom or
  vegetable stock

100g vacuum-packed
  chestnuts, cut in half

small bunch of parsley,
  finely chopped

1 egg, beaten, for sealing
  and brushing

sea salt and black pepper

Pastry

350g plain flour, plus
  extra for dusting

200g butter, chilled

1 egg yolk

sea salt

To make the pastry, put the flour and butter into a food processor with a generous pinch of salt. Pulse until the mixture resembles breadcrumbs. Add the egg yolk and just enough cold water to bind the dough together. Shape the dough into a ball, wrap it in cling film, and chill it in the fridge until you are ready to roll it.

To make the filling, put the butter in a large pan and melt it over a low heat. Add the onion, cover the pan and leave the onion to sweat for 5 minutes. Turn up the heat slightly and add the mushrooms. Cook for a further 4–5 minutes, then add the garlic and herbs.

Add the flour and stir until you can see a paste has formed around the vegetables. Pour in the white wine and stir until it is well incorporated, then add the stock and season with salt and pepper. Bring the mixture to the boil, then turn the heat down and simmer, continuing to stir, until it has thickened. Add the chestnuts and parsley, cover the pan and remove from the heat. Leave to cool. Preheat the oven to 190°C/Fan 170°C/Gas 5.

Divide the pastry into 2 pieces, one slightly bigger than the other. Roll out the larger piece on a lightly floured work surface and use it to line a pie dish, then add the cooled filling. Roll out the remaining pastry and top the pie, wetting the edges with beaten egg and making sure they are well crimped together. Cut a couple of slits in the pie to let steam escape and brush with beaten egg.

Bake the pie in the oven for 40–45 minutes until the crust is golden-brown and the filling is piping hot.

Hairy Biker paella

Sunday dinner is all about sharing food with family and friends, so although paella might not be your usual choice we think it can really fit the bill. It's all in one pot so you can just plonk it on the table and let everyone help themselves. We know there are loads of different recipes and people feel very strongly about them, but this is our version made with fantastic British seafood – our mussels are the best in the world.

Serves 8

1 tbsp olive oil

600g chicken thigh fillets, skinned and diced

150g cooking chorizo, skinned and diced or sliced

4 garlic cloves, crushed

300g large tomatoes, halved, seeded, flesh grated (then skin discarded)

1 tsp sweet smoked paprika

zest of 1 lemon

1.5 litres chicken stock, heated to boiling point

3 bay leaves

2 thyme sprigs

200g green beans, cut into short lengths

500g paella rice

1 tsp saffron threads, soaked in a little warm water

a couple of handfuls of mussels

12 raw king prawns

lemon wedges, to serve

sea salt and black pepper

Heat the oil in a paella pan or a large frying pan over a medium heat. Season the chicken pieces with salt and pepper and fry them for 5 minutes, turning regularly until lightly coloured. Add the chorizo and cook for a further minute.

Add the garlic and cook for another couple of minutes, then push everything to one side. Add the tomatoes and fry them for a few minutes, then mix everything together and sprinkle in the paprika and lemon zest. Pour in all but a large ladleful of the chicken stock and bring back to the boil. Add the bay leaves, thyme and green beans and season with a little salt.

When the chicken stock has come back to the boil, turn the heat down to a simmer and sprinkle in the rice, trying to get it into as even a layer as possible. Pour in the saffron and stir – this is the only time you should stir your paella once the rice has been added! Bring to the boil again, then simmer for 5 minutes.

Turn the heat down and leave the rice to simmer slowly – this should take about 12–15 minutes. If the pan is getting dry, taste the rice – if it's still too firm, add some of the reserved stock and cook for a few more minutes.

Meanwhile, prepare the mussels. Wash them thoroughly, scraping off any barnacles and pulling out the beards. Discard any mussels with broken shells or any that do not close tightly when you tap them sharply.

When you are satisfied the rice is ready, arrange the mussels and prawns over the paella. Cover with a damp tea towel or a lid if you have one and wait for the mussels to steam open and the prawns to turn pink. Serve with lemon wedges.

Scallops with bacon and black pudding

Dave: One time when I stayed at Si's house he cooked me beautiful Scottish scallops with black pudding for Sunday breakfast and it's just as good for Sunday dinner. Sometimes it's nice to have a change and serve something a bit fancy that you wouldn't cook in the week. Scallops aren't cheap but they are a treat and here we eke them out with some bacon and black pudding. All goes down well and even better served with mash.

Serves 4

2 tbsp vegetable oil

8 smoked streaky bacon rashers, rinds removed

25g butter

200g black pudding, cut into 12 thick slices

16 medium-sized scallops, shelled, coral removed and cleaned

100g chicken stock

3 tbsp Marsala

chopped flatleaf parsley, to garnish

sea salt and black pepper

Heat a tablespoon of the oil in a large frying pan. Fry the bacon rashers over a medium-high heat for 4–6 minutes until the fat crisps up, turning them once. If lots of liquid comes out of the bacon, tip it away and return the pan to the heat. Remove the bacon, place it on a baking tray and keep it warm in a low oven.

Heat the remaining oil and a small knob of the butter in the frying pan. Add the black pudding and cook it for 2–3 minutes on each side until it darkens and becomes crisp around the edges, then add it to the tray in the oven. Tip most of the buttery liquid out of the frying pan and return the pan to the hob.

Pat the scallops dry with kitchen paper and season them on both sides with salt and black pepper. Cook them in the frying pan for 1–2 minutes on each side, depending on their size, until golden-brown on the outside but tender within. Take the baking tray out of the oven and put the scallops on it with the bacon and black pudding.

Put the frying pan back on the heat and add the chicken stock and Marsala. Stir well and bring to a simmer. Cut the remaining butter into small pieces, add it to the liquid and stir constantly until the butter melts and the sauce thickens. Remove the pan from the heat.

Serve the scallops with the bacon and black pudding and some mash (see page 266) if you like. Garnish with chopped parsley and drizzle with Marsala sauce.

Duck with orange

Si: This is without doubt one of the world's great dishes. I used to eat at the Hadrian pub in Northumberland a lot and every time I went there I had duck with orange for dinner. It was that good. Here's our version and we've suggested adding kumquats to give a little Hairy Biker twist. Nice with potatoes roasted in duck fat.

Serves 4

————

4 duck breasts
dash of oil or duck fat
sea salt and black pepper

Sauce
50g granulated sugar
12 kumquats, sliced,
　pips removed
200ml red wine
1 tbsp red wine vinegar
2 large shallots,
　finely chopped
2 star anise
2 oranges, juice only
500ml chicken stock

To make the sauce, put the sugar and 50ml of water in a pan and cook over a low heat, stirring regularly, until the sugar has dissolved. Add the kumquats and simmer for about 5 minutes until the kumquats are tender. Remove the kumquats from the syrup and set them aside.

Turn up the heat and boil the syrup until it turns the colour of caramel. Add the red wine, red wine vinegar, shallots and star anise and bring back to the boil. Simmer until the liquid has reduced by half, then add the orange juice and chicken stock.

Again, simmer until the sauce has reduced by half and is rich and syrupy. Taste for seasoning and add salt if necessary and plenty of black pepper. Add the kumquats to the sauce and then set it aside.

For the duck, score a criss-cross pattern through the skin and fat of the duck breasts, stopping just short of the flesh. Sprinkle with salt and pepper. Heat the oil or duck fat in a large frying pan. When it's close to smoking point, add the duck breasts, skin-side down, and fry them until the skin is a rich golden-brown and a great deal of fat has rendered out – this will take 6–7 minutes. Flip the breasts over and sear them for a further 4 minutes. Remove them from the pan and leave them to rest.

Strain off most of the fat from the frying pan, then pour it into the sauce. Deglaze the pan and add back any juices which may have collected under the strained-off fat. Finally add any juices from the resting duck. Simmer until piping hot and very syrupy, then serve the sauce with the sliced duck breasts.

Stuffed chicken breasts

Cumbria meets Umbria in this great recipe that we think makes a perfect Sunday dinner. It looks like a classy restaurant dish but it has lovely traditional flavours. And the good news is that all the prep can be done in advance so you can just pop the parcels in the oven when you're ready. Serve with a green salad or add some roast potatoes for a real feast. This always disappears double quick whenever we cook it and we love it so much we came up with an easy tray bake version (see page 72) for a midweek supper.

Serves 4

4 skinless, boneless
  chicken breasts

175g Cumberland
  sausage meat

2 basil leaves, torn in half

2 sundried tomatoes,
  cut in half

1 tbsp olive oil

juice of ½ lemon

150g Parma ham

sea salt and black pepper

Preheat the oven to 180°C/Fan 160°C/Gas 4. Using a sharp knife, carefully cut a pocket into the side of each chicken breast.

Stuff a quarter of the sausage meat into each chicken pocket and add a piece of basil and sundried tomato.

Drizzle a little olive oil and lemon juice over each chicken breast and season them with salt and pepper. Wrap each breast in some Parma ham to form a neat roll, then wrap each one in foil, sealing the parcels tightly.

Bake in the oven for about 30 minutes. To check the chicken is cooked, carefully unwrap a parcel and pierce the chicken with a metal skewer. If the juices run clear, the meat is cooked all the way through. If they are still pink, put the parcels back for another 5 minutes, then check again. Leave the parcels, still covered, to rest for at least 5 minutes before serving.

Serve the stuffed breasts with the cooking juices from the parcels. They will smell delicious when opened.

Roast chicken with herby stuffing

Roast chicken is the best of all Sunday dinners and brings back so many memories. *Dave*: Roast chicken, called plumpy chicken in our house, takes me back to my childhood, smelling the herby aromas while listening to 'Two-way Family Favourites' on the wireless. *Si*: My mam made the best stuffing and she firmly believed that stuffing belonged in the bird, not in balls.

Serves 4

1.5–1.8kg chicken, trussed and giblets removed

1 onion, thickly sliced

1 parsley sprig

1 thyme sprig

20g butter

½ a lemon

sea salt and black pepper

Stuffing

15g butter

½ onion, finely chopped

2 celery sticks, finely chopped

2 garlic cloves, finely chopped

100g breadcrumbs

zest of 1 lemon

small bunch of parsley, finely chopped

leaves from 2 tarragon sprigs, finely chopped

1 egg

Gravy

1 tbsp flour

100ml white wine

300ml chicken stock

If possible, start preparing the chicken the day before you intend cooking it. Remove the chicken from its packaging. Sprinkle the cavity with flaky sea salt, then place the chicken on a plate. Sprinkle the skin of the chicken with more salt, then cover loosely with kitchen paper and leave it in the fridge. Remove the chicken from the fridge an hour before you want to cook it, so it can come up to room temperature.

To make the stuffing, heat the butter in a frying pan. Add the onion and celery and cook until soft and translucent. Add the garlic and continue to cook for another 2 minutes. Tip everything into a bowl and leave to cool. Add the remaining stuffing ingredients and season with salt and pepper. Mix thoroughly, then spoon the stuffing into the cavity of the chicken. Preheat the oven to 220°C/Fan 200°C/Gas 7.

Weigh the chicken at this point – the cooking time is dependent on the weight once the stuffing is added. The roasting time is 20 minutes for every 500g, plus 15 minutes at a high temperature right at the beginning – see below.

Put the onion and herbs in the centre of a roasting tin and place the chicken on top. Rub the butter over the skin, squeeze over the lemon juice, then put the lemon half in the cavity. Pour 200ml of water around the chicken. Roast at the high temperature for 15 minutes, then turn the heat down to 180°C/Fan 160°C/Gas 4 and continue to cook for the time you have worked out. If you can check with a meat thermometer, the stuffing and the thickest part of the chicken should be 75°C. Or if you pierce the thickest part of a thigh with a skewer, the juices should run clear.

Transfer the chicken and onion to a warm serving platter and loosely cover with foil to rest. Pour off the roasting tin juices into a jug and leave to separate. Strain off any fat. To make the gravy, sprinkle the flour into the roasting tin and place it over a low heat. Stir the flour into the scrapings at the bottom of the tin to form a paste, then pour in the white wine. Allow this to bubble up, then stir until the mixture thickens. Slowly add in the stock and the reserved juices. Strain the liquid into a saucepan and add in any juices from the resting chicken. Bring to the boil then simmer for several minutes. Serve the chicken with the gravy and the stuffing spooned out. Roast potatoes (see page 269) are a must.

Lemon and herb stuffed shoulder of lamb

British lamb is famed for its succulent sweet meat and we particularly enjoy lamb shoulder, as it's tastier and cheaper than leg. A great Sunday dinner with a potato gratin (see page 270).

Serves 6

————

2kg boned lamb shoulder, fat and sinew trimmed

2 tsp extra virgin olive oil

sea salt and black pepper

Stuffing

3 tbsp olive oil

75–100g slightly stale white bread, crusts removed, bread cut into 1cm cubes

1 leek, trimmed and finely sliced

½ onion, finely sliced

4 garlic cloves, crushed

2 tbsp baby capers, drained

zest of 1 lemon

5 heaped tbsp chopped fresh mint

3 heaped tbsp chopped fresh parsley

Gravy

1 heaped tbsp plain flour

300ml lamb stock

1 tbsp redcurrant jelly

few fresh mint sprigs

First make the stuffing. Heat 2 tablespoons of the oil in a large pan. Add the bread cubes, in batches if necessary, and fry them for 3–4 minutes, or until golden-brown, then tip them into a mixing bowl. Add the remaining oil to the pan and add the leek, onion and garlic. Fry them for 2–3 minutes until softened but not browned, then add them to the bowl with the bread. Add the capers, zest, mint and parsley and mix well, then season to taste, with salt and plenty of pepper. Set the stuffing aside to cool.

Preheat the oven to 200°C/Fan 180°C/Gas 6. Place the lamb on a board, skin-side down. Cover it with a sheet of cling film, then use a rolling pen or meat mallet to flatten the meat into a large, neat rectangle, about 3cm thick. Season with salt and pepper.

With the longest sides of the rectangle facing you, spoon the stuffing mixture across the middle of the lamb (from one short side to the other). Wrap the long sides of the lamb rectangle around the stuffing to enclose it. Using butchers' string, tie the lamb securely at 3cm intervals in several places. Tie the ends first, then the middle, then fill in the gaps – that way the stuffing doesn't get squeezed out.

Weigh the lamb joint and put it in a roasting tin, then rub it all over with the oil and season well. Roast the lamb for 20 minutes per every 500g of weight. The full cooking time should be about 1 hour and 20 minutes. When the lamb is cooked to your liking, remove it from the oven and set it on a board. Cover with foil and a couple of clean tea towels to keep it warm, then leave it to rest.

To make the gravy, spoon as much fat as possible from the top of the juices left in the roasting tin, then place the tin over a medium heat and whisk the flour into the juices and cook briefly. Gradually add 300ml of lamb stock to the flour mixture, whisking after each addition until the mixture is smooth and well combined. Stir in the redcurrant jelly and the mint and bring the mixture to a gentle simmer. Continue to simmer for 10 minutes, stirring occasionally, then season to taste. Stir in any juices released from the resting meat, then strain the gravy into a warmed jug.

To serve, trim the ends off the roast lamb parcel, then remove the string. Carve into thick slices and serve with the lamb gravy and mint sauce (see page 273).

Braised steaks with gravy

This is a real old-school British classic and none the worse for that. People often think of braising steak only for stews but if you keep it whole and cook it slowly like this it's full of flavour and really tender. Serve with chips if you like – nothing like chips and good gravy. Get dunking!

Serves 4

4 braising steaks (each about 200g)
3 tbsp vegetable oil
1 onion, cut into 12 wedges
1 garlic clove, crushed
500ml beef stock
1 tbsp tomato purée
leaves from 4–5 thyme sprigs or ½ tsp dried thyme
1 bay leaf
1 tsp cornflour
½ tsp English mustard powder
sea salt and black pepper

Preheat the oven to 160°C/Fan 140°C/Gas 3. Trim any hard fat off the beef and season the meat on both sides with salt and lots of black pepper. Heat a tablespoon of the oil in a large non-stick frying pan.

Fry the steaks, 2 at a time over a medium-high heat for a couple of minutes on each side or until nicely browned. Transfer them to a large flameproof casserole dish. Add a little more oil to the pan in between batches.

Put the pan back on the hob and reduce the heat. Add the remaining oil and gently fry the onion for 5 minutes or until softened and lightly browned, stirring regularly. Stir in the garlic for the last minute of the cooking time.

Add the onion and garlic to the casserole dish, pour over the stock and add the tomato purée. Add the fresh or dried thyme and the bay leaf and stir well. Bring to the boil, then put a lid on the dish and place it in the oven. Cook for 1¼–1½ hours or until the beef is very tender.

Mix the cornflour and mustard powder in a small bowl, then stir in a tablespoon of cold water until smooth. Take the casserole dish out of the oven and stir in the cornflour mixture. Place the dish on the hob over a medium-high heat and simmer for 2–3 minutes until the gravy reduces and becomes thickened and glossy. Serve piping hot with chips (see page 268).

Steak and mushroom pudding

The ultimate in British classics, a good old-fashioned steak pudding just can't be beat. We know some people are a bit iffy about kidneys so we've left them out here and added mushrooms instead. The result is a joy to behold.

Serves 6

———

750g braising steak, cut into 2.5cm pieces

250g portobellini mushrooms, sliced

1 onion, finely chopped

2 tbsp plain flour

1 tsp mustard powder (optional)

leaves from 2–3 large thyme sprigs

1 tbsp tomato purée

200ml red wine

up to 250ml beef stock

sea salt and black pepper

Suet crust

350g self-raising flour

175g suet

butter, for greasing

First make the crust. Put the flour and suet into a bowl and add salt. Add just enough water to make a soft dough – probably about 100ml, but start with 50ml, then increase by the tablespoon. When everything has come together – the texture should be soft and very slightly sticky, not floury – knead the dough very lightly until smooth. Cut a quarter of the dough away to make the lid for the pudding and set it aside. Butter a 1.5-litre pudding basin.

Roll out the remaining pastry into a large round (about the size of a large dinner plate) and use it to line the pudding basin.

To make the filling, put the steak, mushrooms and onion into a large bowl and season with salt and pepper. Mix the flour with the mustard powder, if using, then sprinkle this mixture and the thyme leaves over the steak and mushrooms in the bowl. Combine thoroughly with your hands so everything is covered with the flour.

Tip the steak mixture into the basin and press it down so it is quite tightly packed. Whisk the tomato purée into the wine and pour this over the steak. Add enough stock so the contents of the pudding are covered, with the tops of the meat and mushrooms just poking through.

Roll out the remaining round of pastry. Brush the rim of the pastry covering the basin with water, then place the lid on top. Trim the edges and crimp them together, making sure they are completely sealed. Fold a pleat in the centre of a large piece of foil and place this over the pudding. Fasten the foil in place with string or with a couple of sturdy rubber bands. If your basin is a tight fit inside the pan you are going to be cooking it in, make a string handle for it so it's easy to remove.

Put an upturned saucer or a folded tea towel in the base of a large pan and place the pudding on top. Pour in enough water to reach half way up the pudding basin and cover. Bring to the boil, then turn down to a simmer. Cook for 5 hours, checking at intervals to make sure it isn't boiling dry. Add more boiling water if necessary.

Remove the pudding basin from the pan and set it aside for 5 minutes before removing the foil. Run a palette knife around the edge of the pudding to make sure it is loose enough, then turn it out on to a large serving dish. Serve immediately.

Roast pork with the best crackling

A nice piece of pork is one of the big four roasts – but none of the others have the joy that is crackling! Families have been known to come to blows over getting their fair share. Another reason for choosing this roast for your Sunday dinner is that the pork available now is the best ever – ethically raised and full of flavour. Pure heaven.

Serves 6

1.5–2kg joint of pork, boned and rolled, skin scored
2 tsp olive oil
2 onions, thickly sliced
a few thyme sprigs
3 or 4 star anise (optional)
sea salt and black pepper

Apple sauce

2 large cooking apples, such as Bramleys (about 500g), peeled, cored and sliced
50ml cider or water
2 tbsp soft light brown sugar
25g butter

Gravy

1 tbsp plain flour
100ml cider
400ml pork, chicken or vegetable stock

Preheat the oven to 220°C/Fan 200°C/Gas 7. Make sure the pork skin has been scored. If not, score it now, making sure you cut through the skin to the fat below. A DIY knife is ideal for this task.

Pat the skin dry, then rub it with the oil and sprinkle with salt. Put the onions, thyme and star anise, if using, in a large roasting tin and place the pork on top.

Calculate the cooking time – you need to roast the meat for 30 minutes per 500g. So if you have a joint that weighs 1.5kg, the cooking time should be an hour and a half. Check for doneness after this time – the crackling should be blistered, crisp and brown and the meat should be cooked until the juices run clear or until it has an internal temperature of 63°C.

Meanwhile, make the apple sauce. Put the apples in a pan and add the cider or water, half the sugar and the butter. Cover and cook over a low heat until the apples have broken down into a thick purée. Whisk thoroughly to make sure everything is well combined, then taste and add more sugar if you think the sauce needs it. Spoon the sauce into a serving dish and set it aside until you are ready to eat.

Remove the pork from the oven. Take off the crackling and break it into strips. Transfer the pork to a warm serving dish and cover it with foil. If the crackling isn't crisp enough, put it back in the oven in a smaller tin while the meat rests and you make the gravy.

Strain off the contents of the roasting tin, including most of the fat, and reserve. Discard the onion or add it to the resting pork. Set the roasting tin over a medium heat and sprinkle over the flour. Stir vigorously until the flour has picked up any sticky bits from the base of the tin. Pour in the cider and stir until you have a thick paste. Gradually add the stock and continue to stir until you have a gravy. Pour this into a small saucepan – the base of the roasting tin should be clean.

Bring the gravy to the boil and check the seasoning. Add in any strained meat juices reserved from the roasting tin and from the resting pork. Serve the pork cut into thick slices, with the crackling, gravy and apple sauce.

BELTING BARBECUES AND PICNICS

Classic cheese and onion pie

Dave: Whether for a pie or crisps, cheese and onion is an unbeatable flavour for a picnic – or any time. When I was 18 years old and at college in Lancaster, I used to walk down from the station in the morning and get two cheese and onion pies for breakfast every day. I've loved them ever since and this is our new version of an old favourite, using two great British cheeses.

Serves 4

————

400g waxy potatoes, cut into 1cm dice

1 medium onion, finely chopped

125g Lancashire cheese, coarsely grated

125g mature Cheddar cheese, coarsely grated

1 egg, beaten

sea salt and black pepper

Pastry

350g plain flour, plus extra for dusting

½ tsp baking powder

100g butter

100g lard (or just 200g butter)

1 egg yolk

1 egg, beaten

First make the pastry. Put the flour, baking powder and butter or butter and lard, if using, into a food processor with a generous pinch of salt and pulse until the mixture resembles breadcrumbs. Alternatively, rub the fat into the flour with your fingertips. Add the egg yolk and just enough cold water to bind the dough together. Shape it into 2 discs, one a little larger than the other, then wrap them in cling film and leave them in the fridge until you are ready to roll them.

Next make the filling. Bring a saucepan of salted water to the boil and add the potatoes. Bring the water back to the boil, then cook for 2 minutes. Add the onion and cook for a further minute, then drain thoroughly and set aside to cool. Put the grated cheese into a large bowl and add the cooled potato and onion and the beaten egg. Mix thoroughly and season with salt and pepper.

Preheat the oven to 200°C/Fan 180°C/Gas 6.

Take the smaller of the pastry balls and roll it out on a well-floured surface – use a large dinner plate or cake tin base to cut out a round of about 25cm in diameter. Carefully transfer the disc to a baking tray.

Pile all the filling on to the disc, making sure you leave a border of at least 2cm. Flatten the filling down so it is even – it should be around 2cm high. Roll out the other disc of pastry with any trimmings from the first disc, making sure it is large enough to cover the filling. Brush the edges of the bottom layer of pastry with beaten egg and place the larger one on top, moulding it around the filling. Make sure the edges are well sealed then trim and press a fork around it. Brush the whole pie with beaten egg and cut 2 slits in the centre.

Bake the pie in the preheated oven for 30–35 minutes. Serve hot, straight from the oven, at room temperature, or cold.

Barbecued prawn skewers

We love prawns for a barbie – they taste extra good when cooked over charcoal, it's easy to feed lots of people and they're always a treat. And they're no problem to cook as once they've turned pink you know they're done. Serve with this epic sauce, which also works well with diced mango instead of tomato if you fancy a change.

Serves 4

1 tbsp olive oil

zest of 1 lime

3 garlic cloves, crushed

1 tsp chilli flakes

24 large raw
   shelled prawns

lime wedges, to serve

sea salt and black pepper

Sauce

3 medium tomatoes,
   finely chopped

½ red onion, finely
   chopped

1 fresh red chilli,
   finely chopped

zest and juice of 1 lime

1 tsp red wine vinegar

1 tbsp olive oil

small bunch of coriander,
   finely chopped

leaves from a small bunch
   of mint, finely chopped

First make the marinade by mixing together the olive oil, lime zest, garlic cloves and chilli flakes. Season the prawns with plenty of salt and pepper and add them to the marinade. Mix thoroughly, then cover and leave to marinate for at least half an hour. The prawns can be left in the fridge for up to 24 hours if necessary.

To make the sauce, mix all the ingredients together and season with salt and pepper. If you're using wooden skewers, soak them in cold water first so they don't burn.

To cook the prawns, heat up a barbecue or a griddle pan. Thread the prawns on to skewers and cook them for 2–3 minutes on each side or until they are pink and opaque. Serve the prawns with the sauce and lime wedges for squeezing.

Spicy cheese rolls

Our mission with this idea was to create the most irresistible bread rolls ever – and we think we succeeded. We made them on our 'Comfort Food' show and they just disappeared in seconds. The nice thing about tear-and-share rolls like these is you get the lovely crunchy crust with plenty of soft squidgy insides. Try one, slathered with salty butter, and see if you can resist another. Bet you can't! Ideal for a picnic, so pack some in a basket and go in search of that perfect little patch of grass.

Makes 8–10

500g strong white flour, plus extra for dusting

7g instant yeast

1 tsp salt

1 tsp sugar or honey

2 tbsp olive oil

300ml tepid water

50g chorizo, finely chopped

100g hard cheese (such as Cheddar), grated

2 tbsp finely snipped chives (or finely chopped thyme, oregano, parsley)

1 egg, beaten

Put the flour, yeast, salt and sugar or honey in a bowl and drizzle in the olive oil, then the water. Mix until everything comes together as a dough. Add the chorizo, 50g of the cheese and the chives or other herbs.

Knead the dough in the bowl for a minute to work the additions in a little, then knead on a floured surface until the dough is smooth. Put the dough back in the bowl, cover with a damp cloth or cling film and leave it to rest somewhere warm for 1½ –2 hours, until doubled in size.

Preheat your oven to 220°C/Fan 200°C/Gas 7. Line a 28cm cake tin or a small roasting tin with greaseproof paper. Knock back the dough and divide it into 8–10 even-sized pieces. Knead and shape these into balls, then place them in the prepared tin. Cover with a damp towel again and leave to rise for another 20–30 minutes, or until risen and squashing together.

Brush lightly with the beaten egg (you need a very light touch if the bread dough is at all puffy and springy), then sprinkle over the remaining 50g of cheese. Bake the rolls in the oven for 20–25 minutes, or until cooked through and golden-brown on top. They should feel slightly hollow. Serve warm from the oven or cold.

Salt beef sandwich

This beefy delight is based on the famous Reuben sandwich, which is our very favourite and one we seek out whenever possible. Various people claim to have invented this king among sandwiches but this one is our recipe. It makes enough for one sandwich, including the dressing. Just scale it up to make more and any extra dressing will keep in the fridge. If your meat is at room temperature, not straight from the fridge, it will help the other ingredients warm through and melt the cheese. Great at home and even better outdoors.

Makes 1 sandwich

———————

2 slices of light rye bread or sourdough

butter, for spreading

2–3 slices of salt beef

few slices of Swiss cheese, such as Emmental or Gruyère

2–3 tbsp sauerkraut

dill pickles, to serve

sea salt and black pepper

Dressing

1 tbsp mayonnaise

1 tbsp tomato ketchup

1 tsp horseradish sauce

dash of hot sauce

dash of Worcestershire sauce

1 tsp finely chopped shallot

2 cornichons or ½ dill pickle, finely chopped

pinch of hot paprika

For the dressing, mix all the ingredients together and season with salt and pepper.

Butter both slices of bread. Put the salt beef on one slice, then top with the cheese and sauerkraut. Spread the dressing over the other slice and place it on top of the sauerkraut.

Heat the sandwich in a sandwich maker or in a hot, dry frying pan. If using a frying pan, butter the outsides of both slices of bread, press the sandwich down on to the pan with a spatula, and heat for 3–4 minutes on each side until the bread is well browned and the cheese has melted. Serve with dill pickles.

Tandoori mixed grill

We're always looking for ways to spice up our lives and this is an ace recipe. Everything is prepped and marinated in advance so all you have to do is whack it on the barbie. When we made this on the telly we cooked it on a grill – since they're not keen on you lighting fires in the studio – but at home it goes on the barbecue for that great charcoaly flavour. Easy to do for lots of people – we fed 800 at the Isle of Man TT races in 2007.

Serves 6–8

8 thick lamb cutlets, French trimmed

6 chicken thigh fillets, skinned, flattened out and slashed

12 large raw king prawns, shelled, tail tip left on, deveined

400g salmon fillet, skinned

Marinade

2 tsp ground cardamom

2 tsp ground cumin

2 tsp ground coriander

2 tsp ground turmeric

½ tsp ground cinnamon

¼ tsp ground cloves

grating of nutmeg

2 tbsp Kashmiri chilli powder

½ tsp cayenne

50g fresh root ginger, grated

6 garlic cloves, crushed

500g full-fat yoghurt

juice of 1 lemon

sea salt and black pepper

For the salmon

small bunch of dill, very finely chopped

2 tbsp capers, very finely chopped

Mix all the marinade ingredients together and season with plenty of salt and pepper. Divide it between 4 bowls. Put the lamb in one bowl, chicken in another and the prawns in the third.

Stir the dill and capers into the remaining bowl of marinade and add the salmon. Massage the marinade into the meats, prawns and salmon, then cover and marinate for at least an hour or overnight in the fridge if possible.

When you are ready to cook everything, heat your grill or barbecue to its highest setting. Arrange the chicken on a rack over a lined tray and grill it for 4–5 minutes on each side. Remove and leave it to rest – check that no pinkness remains. Add the lamb and cook it for 2–3 minutes on each side. Again, remove and leave to rest.

The salmon will need 4–5 minutes on each side, then the prawns just 2–3 minutes on each side, depending on their size. You could cook the chicken and salmon together and the lamb and prawns together if you like.

Serve with some naan bread and lemon wedges.

Hairy Biker tip: We like to serve this with a cooling yoghurt dip. Just grate half a peeled cucumber, then squeeze out as much moisture as you can. Stir the grated cucumber into a bowl of natural yoghurt, add some finely chopped mint and season with salt.

The people's pasty

There's a lot of passion about pasties. When we did our 'Food Tour' trip to Cornwall some years back we found out all we could about making the best pasty, then cooked some in the dome at the Eden Centre. We called our recipe The People's Pasty. We've had another look at it and found it was perfect, couldn't be improved on, so here it is. A book of Hairy Biker classics would not be complete without a proper pasty.

Serves 4–6

300g beef skirt (or braising steak), finely chopped

1 tbsp plain flour

450g potato, finely chopped

150g swede, finely chopped

150g onion, finely chopped

1 egg, beaten

sea salt and black pepper

Pastry

450g plain flour, plus extra for dusting

2 tsp baking powder

1 tsp salt

125g butter

2 egg yolks

125ml cold water

For the pastry, blend the flour, baking powder, salt, butter and egg yolks in a food processor until the mixture resembles breadcrumbs. With the motor still running, gradually add the water in a thin stream until the mixture comes together as a dough – you may not need all the water. Wrap the pastry in cling film and chill in the fridge for an hour. Preheat the oven to 180°C/Fan 160°C/Gas 4.

Place the chopped beef and flour in a bowl and mix until the meat is coated in the flour. Season with salt and black pepper, then season all the vegetables.

Divide the pastry into 6 equal pieces. Roll out each piece of pastry on a lightly floured work surface until it is just larger than a dinner plate. Using a dinner plate as a template, trim the edges of each piece of pastry to form a neat disc.

Spoon some of the chopped potato on to one half of each pastry disc, leaving 1.5cm free at the edges. Spoon some of the chopped swede on top of the layer of potato, then add chopped onion. Finally, spoon over some of the beef. Brush the edges of the pastry discs lightly all over with a little of the beaten egg.

Cover the filled side of each pastry disc with the other half of the pastry disc and press the edges together with a fork to seal. Brush the top of each pasty with more beaten egg. Using a sharp knife, cut a small cross shape in the top of the pasties through which the steam can escape.

Place the pasties on a baking tray. Bake for 45–50 minutes, or until the pastry is crisp and golden-brown and the filling is cooked through and piping hot. Set the pasties aside to rest for 5–10 minutes, then serve.

Barbecued belly pork

Dave: One day, not so long ago, I ended up staying at Si's house after a day's work because of a train strike. Kingy got out the barbecue and cooked me this belly pork and I have to say it was the best I'd ever eaten. I had to bin my shirt afterwards though! He'd experimented with different ingredients and come up with this classic Biker recipe – full of flavour to spice up a piece of good British pork.

Serves 4–6

1.5kg belly pork,
skin scored

3 tbsp sea salt

2 star anise, ground

zest of 1 large orange

2 bay leaves

8 garlic cloves

1 tbsp Sichuan
peppercorns

½ tsp Chinese five-spice
powder

200ml olive oil

2 tbsp sesame oil

Make sure your butcher has scored the pork skin well or do it yourself with a small, sharp kitchen knife or a clean DIY knife. Nice fine scores make better crackling. Mix the salt, ground star anise and the orange zest together and rub the mixture well into the skin, making sure the salt goes into all the cuts in the pork rind. Leave the pork overnight in the fridge; do not cover the meat, as you want it to dry.

Using a mini-blender or a pestle and mortar, blend or pound the bay leaves, garlic, peppercorns and five-spice powder to a paste. Slowly add the olive oil and sesame oil while mixing.

Heat a barbecue or griddle and cut the pork into thin slices. Place the pork slices onto the hot griddle or barbecue and brush with the marinade. Cook on each side for a few minutes, or until the meat is cooked through and the skin is crisp.

Pulled pork

OK, this is an American classic but one we need to make our own. One night in Nashville, when filming our 'Mississippi' series, we ended up at a ranch owned by the Sweethearts of the Rodeo – two glamorous ladies from the Grand Ole Opry. Their band included Johnnie Cash's bass player, Dylan's drummer and Bonnie Raitt's guitarist so we were in good company. They played music, we pulled pork and the world seemed a happy place.

Serves 6

2kg boneless pork shoulder

6 white bread rolls

barbecue sauce, to serve

coleslaw, to serve

Dry spice rub

50g soft dark brown sugar

4 tbsp smoked hot paprika

3 tbsp flaked sea salt

1 tbsp cayenne pepper

1 tbsp ground cumin

1 tbsp ground black pepper

1 tbsp dry mustard powder

2 tsp dried thyme

Put all the spice rub ingredients in a bowl and mix well. Place the meat on a board and rub it all over with half the spice mix. Transfer the meat to a shallow dish and cover it loosely with cling film, then leave in the fridge for 1–2 hours. Reserve the remaining rub.

Take the pork out of the dish and put it on a board. Massage with the remaining dry rub. Preheat the oven to 150°C/Fan 130°C/Gas 2.

Stand the pork on a rack in a roasting tin, skin-side up. Pour 100ml of water into the tin and cover the pork and tin with a large piece of foil, pinching the foil around the edges to make a good seal. Put the pork in the oven and cook it for 5 hours.

To finish it off on the barbecue (optional): 30 minutes before the pork is ready, light at least 2kg of lumpwood charcoal in a kettle barbecue according to the manufacturer's directions. When the barbecue coals are hot and have a light coating of ash, push them to one side and put the pork, either in its tin (with the liquid drained) or in a foil tray, directly on the barbecue.

Add a couple of handfuls of soaked wood chips as directed on the packet instructions (either to a foil dish or directly on the coals) and close the lid.

Barbecue the pork for a further 45 minutes until the smoke and heat forms a crust all over the meat. It should look a very dark reddish-brown and even a little blackened in places. Occasionally, check that the pork's internal temperature remains at least 75°C. If the smoke dies down or the coals lose their heat, add a few more coals, cover with the lid and continue cooking.

When the pork is cooked, transfer it to a board, cover with a sheet of foil and leave to stand for 15 minutes. Pull the meat into shreds with a couple of forks. To serve, split the bread rolls and fill them with the hot pork. Serve with barbecue sauce, or hot sauce, and some coleslaw.

Classic burgers

There's no way we could leave burgers out of this book. We've cooked 'em all – buffalo, zebra even veggie – but this recipe can't be beat. The secret is to use chuck steak, not mince, and chill it well so you can chop it perfectly. The result is a beautifully juicy burger. We love the bone marrow which we think makes burger perfection, but we've added an option of using bacon fat instead if you like. And don't forget that these make great juicy lucys – burgers with the cheese in the middle instead of on top.

Serves 4

———

800g chuck steak, trimmed of any gristle or hard pieces of fat

50g bone marrow, finely diced (optional)

4 burger buns, split

sea salt and black pepper

Burger sauce

100g mayonnaise

2 tbsp tomato ketchup

a squeeze of lemon juice

1 large gherkin, finely chopped

1 tsp garlic powder

½ tsp chipotle paste or other hot sauce

First prepare the meat. Make sure it's well chilled – in fact, you can freeze the meat, then let it thaw partially and you'll find it much easier to cut. Put the meat through a coarse mincer, or chop it very finely by hand. It should be fine enough to stick together when you squeeze a handful. Add the bone marrow, if using.

Season the mixture with salt and a little black pepper, then divide the mixture into 4 and shape into round patties 2–2.5cm thick. The mincing and chopping will help bring the meat to room temperature, but if not, leave the burgers to stand for a while.

Heat a non-stick frying pan or your barbecue. When the pan or grill is too hot to hold your hand over, add the burgers – there's no need for oil, as some fat will render out of the meat. Leave for 4 minutes, by which time the burgers should be very well seared and have a thick crust. Flip them and cook for another 3 minutes for rare meat, 4 minutes for medium-rare, 5 for medium and up to 6 for well done.

If you want a cheesy topping, add some once you've flipped the burgers.

Once the burgers are cooked to your liking, leave them to rest for a couple of minutes. Meanwhile, put the burger buns cut-side down on the pan or barbecue to toast very slightly and take up some of the meat flavours. Serve with your choice of toppings.

To make the burger sauce, mix all the ingredients together and season with salt and black pepper.

Hairy Biker tip: If you would like to try these with bacon instead of bone marrow, fry 4 rashers of streaky bacon slowly in a pan to render as much fat as possible. Allow the fat to cool, then add it to your burger mixture. Use the bacon rashers to garnish your burgers.

Fruity flapjacks

Dave: Flapjacks are one of the first things I ever cooked, baking them in the old trays that toffee used to come in when I was a lad. I never was a cream cake fan – these are my sweet treats and the stickier and softer the better. Everyone loves a tray bake and these classic flapjacks are so easy to wrap up and pop in your picnic basket.

Makes 10

300g unsalted butter

100g golden syrup OR
  75g golden syrup and
  25g maple syrup

100g light soft
  brown sugar

100g pitted dates, chopped

pinch of salt

500g porridge oats

100g raisins

100g glacé cherries

100g chopped pecans

Preheat your oven to 190°C/Fan 170°C/Gas 5. Line a 20 x 30cm baking tin with non-stick baking paper.

Put the butter, golden syrup (and maple syrup, if using), sugar and dates into a large saucepan. Add a pinch of salt. Melt over a very low heat, stirring at intervals until the sugar has dissolved.

Remove the pan from the heat and add the remaining ingredients, stirring thoroughly until everything is well combined. Press the mixture firmly and evenly into the prepared tin.

Bake in the oven for 25–30 minutes, depending on whether you want your flapjacks chewy or crunchy.

Remove from the oven and leave for several minutes before cutting into slices, then leave to cool completely in the tin. Store in an airtight container for up to a week.

TASTY
TEATIME

Potted cheese with bacon

This is a cheese spread that's fit for a queen and it's perfect on crusty bread or with a teatime cracker. We've come a long way from those little cheese triangles we used to love as kids – although we still enjoy them once in a while! Best to use a fairly mild Cheddar for this or the flavour will overpower everything else.

Serves 4

175g butter
100g smoked back bacon,
    rinds removed
1 shallot, finely chopped
125g Cheddar
    cheese, grated
1 tsp fresh thyme leaves
2 tbsp sherry
½ tsp mustard powder

First clarify the butter. Put it in a small saucepan over a gentle heat and allow it to melt. When it starts foaming, skim off the foam until you can see how the butter has separated into 2 distinct layers. Strain off the clear layer into a separate container, then discard the milky layer left in the pan.

Put a tablespoon of the clarified butter into a frying pan. Add the bacon and cook until crisp and well browned in places, then remove it and set aside. Add the shallot and a little more butter if necessary, then fry it over a medium-high heat until softened and well caramelised. Remove the pan from the heat.

Finely chop the bacon and reserve a couple of tablespoons – also reserve a teaspoon of the fried shallot. Put the remaining bacon and shallot in a food processor and pulse until it has all broken down to a paste.

Add the cheese, thyme leaves, sherry, mustard powder and 50ml of the clarified butter to the food processor. Keep processing until you have a fairly smooth paste, stopping to scrape down the sides of the bowl when necessary. When you have a smooth paste, stir in the reserved bacon and shallot.

Transfer the mixture to a bowl and cover with the rest of the clarified butter. Cover the bowl with cling film and store in the fridge.

Quiche lorraine

The name is French but actually this is good old egg and bacon tart and it's as much of a classic in Britain as in France. We wanted to get to the source of the quiche so we travelled to Alsace, where we baked our recipe near a monument to the fallen of World War II. We were overlooking a vineyard so we enjoyed a glass of local wine with our quiche – simply perfect. This is proof that real men, women, boys and girls all eat quiche. This makes a lovely teatime dish but it's great at any time of day.

Serves 6

---

1 tbsp olive oil

1 onion, finely sliced

200g smoked streaky
   bacon, cut into
   2cm pieces

300ml double cream

200ml crème fraiche

3 large eggs

75g Gruyère cheese,
   grated

sea salt and black pepper

Pastry

250g plain flour, plus
   extra for dusting

150g cold butter,
   cut into cubes

1 large egg, beaten

To make the pastry, put the flour and butter in a food processor and pulse until the mixture resembles breadcrumbs. Add the beaten egg and mix until the mixture is just beginning to come together, then shape the dough into a ball.

Roll out the pastry on a lightly floured surface to the thickness of a pound coin. Place the pastry in a 23cm loose-based tart tin, pressing it well into the sides. Trim away any excess pastry and lightly prick the base. Leave the pastry case to chill in the fridge for 30 minutes. Preheat the oven to 200°C/Fan 180°C/Gas 4.

Take the tin out of the fridge, place a piece of baking paper over the pastry and fill it with baking beans. Put the tin on a baking tray and bake the pastry for 25 minutes. Remove the paper and beans and bake for another 5–10 minutes. Remove from the oven and turn the temperature down to 170°C/Fan 150°C/Gas 3½.

Heat the oil in a frying pan and fry the onion and bacon together until lightly browned, stirring regularly. Tip them on to a plate and leave to cool. Put the cream, crème fraiche and eggs in a jug and beat until well combined, then season with salt and pepper.

Spoon the bacon and onion into the pastry case and spread it evenly, then scatter the cheese on top. Slowly pour in most of the egg mixture, then place the tin, on the baking tray, in the oven. Pull out the oven shelf slightly and pour the rest of the egg mixture into the pastry case, then gently push the shelf back in. This method is much easier than trying to carry a very full tin to the oven!

Bake for 35–40 minutes until the filling is just beginning to brown and has lost its wobble. If you press the back of a teaspoon on to the centre, no liquid should be visible. Take the quiche out of the oven and leave it to cool in the tin for 15 minutes before removing. Serve warm or cold.

Welsh rarebit

When you're cold, tired and hungry, nothing beats this posh cheese on toast. The mustard, Worcestershire sauce and beer give such a punchy flavour and we're not averse to piling a couple of slices of bacon on the top. Or you can add some ham and call it a Welsh croque-madame! A great teatime treat.

Serves 4

———

25g butter

25g plain flour

100ml strong, dark beer

150g mature Cheddar cheese, grated

1 egg yolk

1 tsp English mustard

4 tsp Worcestershire sauce

pinch of cayenne pepper (optional)

4 thick slices of wholemeal or granary bread

black pepper

Preheat the grill to high. Melt the butter in a non-stick pan and stir in the flour. Cook over a low heat for 30 seconds, stirring constantly, then slowly add the beer. Simmer for 2–3 minutes, stirring all the time until the sauce is thick and smooth.

Add the cheese, egg yolk, mustard, Worcestershire sauce and cayenne pepper, if using, then cook until the cheese melts, stirring constantly. Season with black pepper, remove the pan from the heat and set aside to cool.

Place the bread on a baking tray lined with foil and toast it on each side until golden-brown. Spread the cheese sauce thickly over the bread, making sure the slices are completely covered so the edges don't burn. Put them under the hot grill for 20–30 seconds more until lightly browned and bubbling.

Cheese and tomato chutney turnovers

Si: Roll me over, lay me down and give me another of these top turnovers. Cheese and chutney are a great British combo and these really hit the spot when we cooked them for our 'Comfort Food' series. We suspect that some of the crew still have tomato stains in their trouser pockets.

Serves 6

———

375g self-raising flour,
   plus extra for dusting

½ tsp fine sea salt

75g cold butter,
   cut into cubes

225ml whole milk

180g Somerset brie

6 heaped tbsp
   tomato chutney

300ml vegetable oil,
   for frying

To make the pastry, put the flour and salt into a bowl and rub in the butter with your fingertips until the mixture resembles coarse breadcrumbs. Slowly add the milk, stirring constantly until the mixture comes together and forms a soft, spongy dough. Knead lightly and form into a ball.

Roll out half the dough on a lightly floured surface until it's about 3mm thick. Take a saucer, or an upturned bowl, about 14cm in diameter and cut around it to make 3 circles of dough, re-kneading and rolling the dough if necessary. Repeat with the remaining dough so you have 6 circles.

Remove and discard the rind from the cheese and cut the cheese into small chunks. Spoon a heaped tablespoon of chutney into the middle of each round of pastry spreading it out but leaving a 1cm border all around the edge.

Place a sixth of the cheese on one side of each circle. Brush the edges of the dough with a little water. Fold over to encase the filling, pushing out any air, and press the edges together. Press the tines of a fork around the edge of the pastry, pressing firmly through both layers, to ensure that the pie is sealed.

Pour the oil into a large frying pan – it should be about 1cm deep. Place over a medium heat and leave until the oil is about 150°C or hot enough to brown a cube of white bread in 15 seconds. Do not allow the oil to overheat and do not leave the oil unattended. You can use a deep-fat fryer if you prefer.

Using a spatula, place a couple of turnovers into the hot oil and cook for about 2 minutes on each side, or until lightly browned and slightly puffed up. The cheese inside will be lovely and melted when the turnovers are cut open. If the oil is too hot, the pastry will brown too much before the filling is ready. Remove the turnovers, cover with foil and keep them warm while you cook the rest.

The turnovers can also be made in advance and reheated in a hot oven for about 10 minutes if you like.

Fruit scones

Oh my, oh my – how many scones have we baked in our career! Scones with fruit, cheese scones, scones with maple syrup and pecans or white chocolate and cranberry – you name it, we've sconed it. Here, we're giving you the classic scone for teatime perfection. Going, going, scone – these don't hang around, we can tell you. The big question with scones is – jam first or cream first? We're both jam-first people.

Makes 8–12

400g self-raising flour,
  plus extra for dusting
1 tsp baking powder
50g caster sugar
pinch of salt
125g butter, chilled
  and diced
100g sultanas or raisins
2 eggs, beaten
100ml milk

Preheat the oven to 220°C/Fan 200°C/Gas 7.

Put the flour, baking powder and caster sugar into a bowl with a generous pinch of salt. Add the butter and rub it in with your fingertips until the mixture resembles very fine breadcrumbs.

Stir in the sultanas or raisins. Reserve a tablespoon of the beaten eggs, then add the rest to the dry ingredients along with the milk. Mix until everything comes together to form a dough. If the dough is too crumbly, add a little more milk.

Turn the dough out on to a floured work surface and knead it very gently until smooth. Roll the dough out to a thickness of about 2cm and cut out rounds. For large scones use a 7.5cm cutter, for smaller ones, use a 6cm cutter. Make sure you press the cutter firmly down through the dough and remove it without twisting if you want perfectly straight-sided scones. Re-roll the trimmings until you have used all the dough.

Place the scones on a large baking tray, spacing them well apart, then brush them with the reserved beaten egg. Bake them in the oven for 10–12 minutes, until well risen and a light golden brown. Remove the scones from the oven and place them on a wire rack to cool.

Victoria sponge with blackberries and spiced cream

The WI will be proud of us for this recipe and, though we say it ourselves, it is absolutely gorgeous and tastes as good as it looks. The cream and blackberries bring a touch of something special to this very traditional British cake, and you can add a splash of blackberry liqueur for an extra hit of fruitiness if you like.

Makes 10–12 slices

Sponge cakes
225g butter, softened
225g caster sugar
4 eggs
225g self-raising flour
2 tbsp lemon juice

Blackberries
150g blackberries
1 tbsp caster sugar
1 tbsp blackberry liqueur, such as crème de mûre (optional)

Spiced cream
250ml double or whipping cream
2 tbsp icing sugar
½ tsp ground cardamom
¼ tsp ground allspice
¼ tsp ground cinnamon
¼ tsp ground mace

Preheat the oven to 180°C/Fan 160°C/Gas 4. Butter and line 2 x 20cm sandwich tins. Using a hand-held electric whisk or a stand mixer, cream the butter and sugar together until very light and fluffy – it should be almost mousse-like. This will take a good 5 minutes.

Add the eggs, one at a time, with a tablespoon of the flour, mixing lightly in between each addition, then add the rest of the flour. Add as much lemon juice as you need to achieve a dropping consistency, then divide the mixture between the 2 tins.

Bake the cakes in the oven for 20–25 minutes, or until the sponge has shrunk away from the sides slightly, is springy to the touch and a very light golden-brown. Leave the cakes to cool in the tins for at least 10 minutes, then turn them out on to a cooling rack.

For the filling, put the blackberries in a bowl and sprinkle over the caster sugar and blackberry liqueur, if using. Leave the berries to marinate for a short while – they will give out some juices.

For the spiced cream, whip the cream in a bowl to just beyond soft peak stage, then fold in the icing sugar and spices.

To assemble, pile the spiced cream on to one of the sponges. Top with the blackberries and pour over any juices. Place the remaining sponge on top. Dust with icing sugar or caster sugar and serve.

Hairy Biker tip: You could use spelt flour instead of ordinary flour for a slightly nutty flavour that works really well with blackberries. If you do, add 2 teaspoons of baking powder to the flour.

Gingerbread cake

If you can, wrap up this spicy teatime treat and keep it for a few days before eating – just like us, it gets better with age! We think it's one of our best-ever cake recipes. The love of ginger and other spices in the UK goes back to Tudor days and we think this recipe is one you'll return to time and time again. *Dave*: This is a real Lakes classic and as good as the one my Auntie Mary used to make.

Serves 8

300g plain flour

2 tbsp ground ginger (or to taste – this makes for quite a hot cake)

½ tsp cayenne pepper

½ tsp ground cinnamon

½ tsp ground allspice

¼ tsp mace

generous pinch of ground cloves

150g butter

125g dark brown muscovado sugar

150g golden syrup

1 jar of stem ginger

200g black treacle

250ml milk

1 heaped tsp bicarbonate of soda

2 large eggs, lightly beaten

Preheat the oven to 170°C/Fan 150°C/Gas 3½. Line a 30 x 20cm tin with baking paper – a straight-sided brownie tin is just right.

Sift the flour into a large bowl, add the spices and mix lightly to combine.

Put the butter, sugar, golden syrup, 50g of the syrup from the jar of stem ginger and the treacle into a pan, place over a gentle heat and allow everything to melt together.

Remove the pan from the heat and whisk in the milk, bicarbonate of soda and eggs. Gradually add the contents of the pan to the flour, making sure everything is well combined, and you will have a very wet, pourable batter. Drain the balls of stem ginger and rinse them, then chop them finely. Stir the chopped stem ginger into the batter.

Pour the batter into the prepared tin and bake in the oven for 45–60 minutes. When the edges of the gingerbread have pulled back slightly from the side of the tin and the top is springy to touch, it will be done.

Cool in the tin for half an hour and then turn it out on to a wire rack. Ideally, wrap the gingerbread and keep it for a few days before eating – the gingerbread's stickiness will develop as it matures.

Hairy Biker tips: To make it easier to spoon out syrup and treacle, oil the spoon first and the syrup or treacle will just slide off.

If you don't have any stem ginger, leave it out and use an extra 50g of golden syrup instead of the stem ginger syrup.

Biker brownies

Brownies are one of the all-time great teatime classics. These are easy to make and pimped up with choc spread and hazelnuts to make something totally irresistible. They're great with a cup of tea in front of the telly or warm with a scoop of vanilla ice cream. Fudgy and fantastic.

Makes 12

100g plain flour
50g cocoa powder
¾ tsp baking powder
pinch of salt
300g dark chocolate (minimum 70% cocoa solids)
250g butter
250g granulated sugar
4 eggs
100g hazelnuts, roughly chopped
100g chocolate hazelnut spread (optional)
50ml hazelnut liqueur (optional)

Preheat the oven to 170°C/Fan 150°C/Gas 3½. Line a 30 x 20cm straight sided brownie tin with foil or non-stick baking paper.

Sift the flour, cocoa and baking powder together in a bowl and add a good pinch of salt. Break 250g of the chocolate into a heatproof bowl and place the bowl over a pan of barely simmering water. Make sure the bottom of the bowl does not touch the water. Leave the chocolate to melt, stirring regularly.

When the chocolate has melted, remove the bowl and leave the chocolate to cool slightly. Roughly chop the remaining chocolate and set it aside.

Beat the butter and sugar together in a bowl until very light and fluffy. Add the eggs, one at a time, then pour in the melted chocolate. Mix thoroughly, then add a third of the flour mixture. Stir to combine, then repeat with the other two-thirds of flour. Add half the hazelnuts and all the reserved chopped chocolate and stir to combine. Scrape the mixture into the prepared tin.

If using the chocolate spread and hazelnut liqueur, mix them together to make a smooth paste. Make little wells in the brownie batter and add spoonfuls of the mixture.

Sprinkle the remaining hazelnuts on top and press them down lightly. Bake in the preheated oven for about 30 minutes, testing after 25 minutes. When the brownies are done, a wooden skewer should come out with a few crumbs attached – it shouldn't be wet, but it shouldn't be completely clean either.

Leave the brownies to cool in the tin. If you can bear to wait, put the tin in the fridge overnight to rest the brownies before cutting them – it will help them settle into a consistency that isn't too cake-like. Cut into squares or triangles and store them in an airtight tin.

Lemon and blueberry muffins

Buoyed by the success of the microwave lemon and blueberry mug cakes in our latest Hairy Dieters' book, we decided to develop a full-fat version. Blueberries are in British supermarkets all year round now and when paired with zingy lemons they make a flavour combo that we just can't get enough of. So when you're feeling that teatime temptation – stuff in a muffin.

Makes 12

100g butter
250g self-raising flour
1 tsp bicarbonate of soda
100g golden caster sugar, plus 2 tsp for sprinkling
100g blueberries
grated zest of 1 lemon
2 eggs
150ml natural yoghurt
2 tbsp milk
12 tsp lemon curd

Preheat the oven to 200°C/Fan 180°C/Gas 6. Line a 12-hole deep muffin tin with paper cases.

Melt the butter in a small pan over a low heat, then set it aside to cool for a few minutes.

Sift the flour and bicarbonate of soda into a large bowl and stir in the 100g of sugar, the blueberries and lemon zest. Make a well in the centre.

Beat the eggs in a bowl with a large whisk until smooth, then beat in the yoghurt, milk and melted butter until well combined. Stir this into the flour mixture with a large metal spoon until very lightly combined. Don't overwork the mixture.

Divide the batter between the muffin cases. Place a teaspoon of lemon curd on top of each one and sprinkle with the remaining sugar. Bake for 20 minutes or until well risen and golden-brown.

Serve the muffins warm or leave them to cool on a wire rack. The lemon curd will be very hot, so don't be tempted to eat these as soon as they come out of the oven or you'll burn your tongue!

Dundee cake

This is one of our favourite cakes and we're in good company – the Queen is said to like a slice of Dundee cake at teatime. It was first made in the nineteenth century by Keiller's, the marmalade company based in Dundee, and is lovely served with a hunk of cheese and a hot cup of tea. Dundee cake is not hard to make and we find the task of arranging the blanched almonds on top strangely satisfying.

Serves 10

175g softened butter,
  plus extra for greasing
175g soft light
  brown sugar
3 tbsp orange marmalade
3 eggs, beaten
225g self-raising flour
25g ground almonds
1 heaped tsp
  ground mixed spice
400g mixed dried fruit
75g glacé cherries, halved
2 tbsp whisky or milk
60g blanched almonds,
  to decorate
1 tsp granulated or caster
  sugar, to decorate

Preheat the oven to 150°C/Fan 130°C/Gas 2. Grease a 20cm loose-bottomed cake tin and line it with a double layer of baking paper.

Beat the butter and sugar in a food processor or with a hand-held electric whisk for 3–4 minutes, or until very light and fluffy.

Add the marmalade and mix for a few seconds more. Slowly add the eggs, one at a time, beating well after each addition.

Add the flour, almonds and spices to the batter. Mix slowly until well combined, then stir in the mixed dried fruit and cherries with a large metal spoon. Add the whisky or milk and mix until well combined.

Spoon the mixture into the cake tin, smooth the surface and carefully arrange the blanched almonds in circles on top.

Bake the cake for 1½–2 hours, or until it's well risen, firm and golden-brown. Test the cake by inserting a skewer into the centre. If the skewer comes out clean, the cake is done. Leave the cake to cool for 10 minutes, then remove it from the tin, peel off the paper and set aside to cool on a wire rack.

Sprinkle the top of the cake with granulated sugar. Store it in a cake tin and eat within 4–5 days – that shouldn't be hard!

Carrot and sultana cake with orange frosting

Who doesn't love a carrot cake? Carrots have a natural sweetness and they bring great flavour and moistness to a bake. We've taken a classic and made it into a good old British tray bake that's dead easy to put together. And the orange frosting really takes it to another level of deliciousness.

Makes 12

200g self-raising flour

75g sultanas

75g pecans, broken
  into rough pieces

grated zest of ½ orange

1 tsp ground cinnamon

½ whole nutmeg,
  finely grated

1 tsp baking powder

½ tsp bicarbonate of soda

pinch of fine sea salt

3 eggs

175ml sunflower oil,
  plus extra for greasing

175g soft light
  brown sugar

200g carrots, grated

Cream cheese icing

100g icing sugar

100g unsalted butter,
  softened

1 tsp fresh orange juice

200g full-fat cream cheese

grated zest of ½ orange

25g pecan nuts,
  roughly broken

Preheat the oven to 180°C/Fan 160°C/Gas 4. Grease a 20cm square, loose-bottomed cake tin and line it with baking paper.

Place the flour, sultanas, pecans, orange zest, cinnamon, grated nutmeg, baking powder, bicarb and salt in a large bowl and mix until well combined.

Beat the eggs in a separate bowl until smooth. Add the sunflower oil and sugar and whisk until well combined.

Make a well in the centre of the flour mixture and beat in the wet ingredients until smooth. Stir in the carrots. Pour the mixture into the prepared cake tin and smooth the surface. Bake in the centre of the oven for 35–40 minutes, until the cake is well risen and feels springy to the touch. Test by inserting a skewer into the centre. If the skewer comes out clean, the cake is done.

Remove the cake from the oven and set it aside to cool in the tin for 5 minutes. Then remove the cake from the tin and leave it on a wire rack to cool completely.

For the icing, sift the icing sugar into a large bowl and add the butter and orange juice. Beat together with a large wooden spoon until light and creamy. Add the cream cheese and orange zest and beat until smooth. Cover and chill in the fridge for 30 minutes or until firm enough to spread.

Spread the icing over the cooled cake and sprinkle with the pecans. Cut into 12 pieces to serve.

Madeira cake

Si: My auntie Hilda used to make a Madeira cake every other day so there was always some at her house for tea. I used to call it rice cake for some reason and it was dead good, even better spread with a nice bit of jam. The texture makes it great for a trifle too.

Serves 8

250g butter, softened,
  plus extra for greasing

300g plain flour

2 tsp baking powder

pinch of salt

200g caster sugar

zest and juice of
  2 clementines,

3 eggs

2 tbsp caster sugar,
  for the topping

Preheat the oven to 170°C/ Fan 150°C/Gas 3½. Grease a large 900g loaf tin and line it with baking paper.

Mix the flour, baking powder and salt in a bowl. Using hand-held electric beaters, beat together the butter, caster sugar and clementine zest in a separate bowl. Add the eggs, one at a time, to the butter and sugar mixture, sprinkling over a couple of tablespoons of flour with each addition and mixing well.

Fold in the rest of the flour followed by the clementine juice. The texture will be slightly firmer than the dropping consistency you need for a lighter sponge.

Scrape the batter into the prepared tin and sprinkle the caster sugar on top. Bake the cake in the oven for 55–60 minutes, or until a cake skewer comes out clean. The cake will be a rich golden-brown and may have cracked lengthways down the middle – this is normal for a Madeira cake.

Remove the cake from the oven and leave to cool in the tin for 5 minutes, before transferring it to a wire rack to finish cooling. Store in an airtight tin.

Chocolate and cherry buns

Wow – this is a variation on a classic chelsea bun that's got all done up for a party. Of all the sweet things we've ever made on set, we've never seen anything disappear so fast. They're naughty but very, very nice.

Makes 10–12 buns

75g butter, plus extra
for greasing
250ml milk
500g strong white
bread flour
1 tsp mixed
spice (optional)
7g instant yeast
75g soft light brown sugar
pinch of salt
1 egg
vegetable oil, for greasing

Filling
100g butter, softened
50ml maple syrup
25g dark soft brown sugar
1 tsp ground cinnamon
1 tsp ground mixed spice
pinch of salt
100g glacé cherries,
halved
100g chocolate chips

To bake
1 egg, beaten
2 tbsp demerara sugar

For the glaze (optional)
1–2 tbsp just-boiled water
200g icing sugar

Line a 26–28cm deep cake tin or a deep roasting tin with baking paper and grease it generously with butter.

Put the milk in a saucepan, place it over a gentle heat and bring it to just below boiling point. Remove the pan from the heat and add the butter, then set aside until the butter has melted and the mixture has cooled to blood temperature.

Put the flour and mixed spice, if using, in a large bowl and add the yeast, sugar and a pinch of salt. Make a well in the middle.

Beat the egg into the milk and butter mixture. Add this to the flour and stir until well combined – it will be a very soft, sticky dough.

Lightly oil your hands and the work surface, then turn out the dough. Knead until the dough is no longer sticky and has become smooth and elastic. Put the dough back in the bowl and cover it with a damp tea towel, then leave it to rise until doubled in size. This will take about an hour and a half.

For the filling, beat the butter with the maple syrup, sugar, spices and a pinch of salt to make a creamy, toffee-coloured mixture.

Turn the dough out and roll or pat it into a rectangle of about 30 x 23cm. Spread the butter mixture over the dough, then sprinkle with the chocolate chips and cherries. Roll the dough up fairly tightly, then cut it into 10–12 pieces.

Arrange the rounds, cut-side down, in the deep cake tin. Brush them with some of the beaten egg, then leave for another 30 minutes. Preheat the oven to 180°C/Fan 160°C/Gas 4. Brush with egg again, then sprinkle with the sugar. Bake the buns in the oven for 20–25 minutes, or until they are a rich golden-brown and well risen.

For the optional glaze, gradually add enough just-boiled water to the icing sugar to make a glaze that's thin enough to pour, but won't run off too much. Leave the buns to cool in the tin, then drizzle over the glaze. Leave to set.

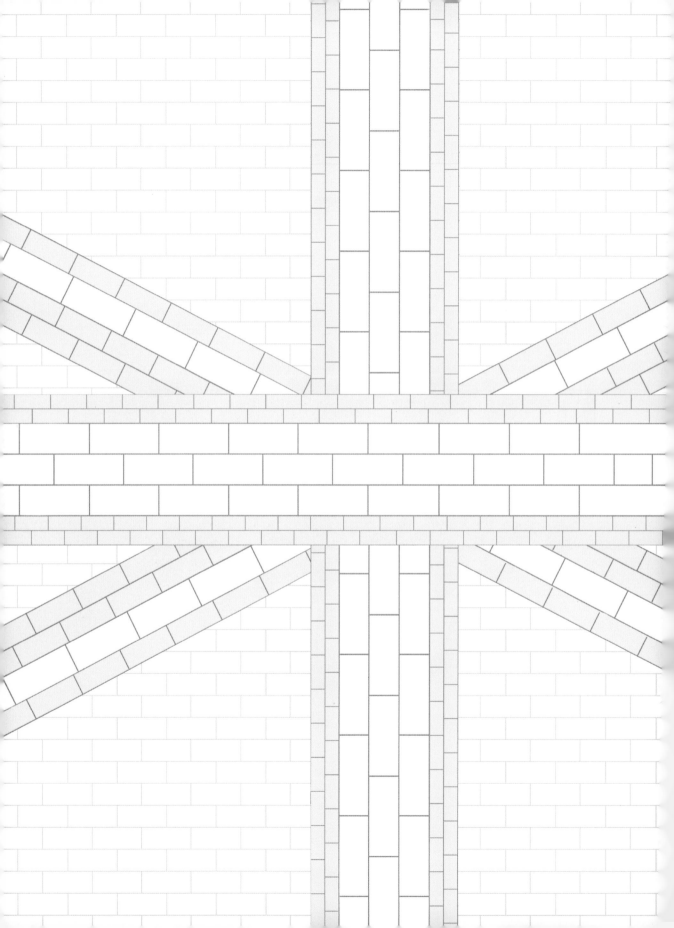

PERFECT
PUDDINGS

Mississippi mud pie, Biker style

Whether via the Mississippi or Mersey, this has become a British favourite and a Biker classic. It's a recipe we discovered on our trip to the southern US a few years ago and it is the most indulgent dessert ever. If you want a big bruiser of a pud for a special occasion, this is the one for you. No way we could leave it out of this book.

Serves 8

Base and sides
75g butter

150g chocolate
   digestive biscuits

150g dark chocolate
   sandwich biscuits

Filling
135g plain dark chocolate,
   broken into squares

135g butter, cubed

3 large eggs

150g light soft
   brown sugar

25g cocoa powder, sifted

150ml double cream

Topping
500ml double cream

1 tbsp light soft
   brown sugar

25g plain dark
   chocolate, grated

Ideally, make this in a metal pie dish with sloping sides for the best results. The dish should measure about 23cm in diameter at the top with a base of about 18cm. Line the dish with foil to make it easier to remove the pie once it's cooked.

First make the mixture for the base and sides. Melt the butter in a small pan. Break the biscuits into chunky pieces and put them in a food processor. Blitz them into crumbs, then add the melted butter and, with the motor running, blend until thoroughly mixed.

Sprinkle the crumbs into the pie dish and press them firmly into the base and sides. Make sure the biscuit base is evenly distributed, especially where the base meets the sides. Put the dish on a small baking tray and chill it in the fridge for 30 minutes.

Now for the filling. Put the chocolate and butter into a heatproof bowl and place the bowl over a pan of simmering water, making sure the bottom of the bowl doesn't touch the water. Leave the chocolate and butter to melt, stirring occasionally. Remove the bowl from the pan and set it aside to cool for 10 minutes. Preheat the oven to 180°C/Fan 160°C/Gas 4.

Using an electric hand-held whisk, beat the eggs and sugar together in a large bowl until very light and creamy. They should roughly triple in volume.

Whisk in the chocolate mixture in a steady stream, then whisk in the sifted cocoa powder and the cream until well combined.

Pour the mixture into the prepared biscuit base and bake the pie for 35–40 minutes until it is just firm and slightly risen. Leave it to cool in the tin. The pie filling will sink a little as it cools. When the pie is cold, carefully remove it from the tin and slide it off the foil and on to a serving plate. Chill it in the fridge for at least an hour before serving.

For the topping, whisk the cream with the sugar until very soft peaks form. Spoon the cream on to the pie in generous peaks. Sprinkle with the grated chocolate and serve.

Apple and blackberry pie

A proper apple pie is a real treat but apple and blackberry is even better and brings back memories of searching the hedgerows for blackberries when we were lads. Of course you can get blackberries in the supermarket, but we like the idea of coming home with stained fingers and a bag of blackberries, then making this pie. A true British classic that just can't be bettered.

Serves 6

————

150g golden caster sugar, plus 1 tbsp for sprinkling

1 tsp ground cinnamon

2 tbsp cornflour

600g Bramley cooking apples, peeled, cored and sliced

200g blackberries

1 egg, beaten

Pastry

400g plain flour, plus extra for dusting

2 tbsp caster sugar

grated zest of 1 lemon

250g cold butter, cut into cubes

1 egg, beaten with 2 tbsp cold water

For the pastry, put the flour, sugar, lemon zest and butter into a food processor and pulse until the mixture resembles fine breadcrumbs. Gradually add the beaten egg and water and mix until the mixture forms a rough ball. Tip the pastry on to a floured surface and set one-third aside for the pie lid.

Roll out the remaining pastry on a floured surface until it's the thickness of a pound coin and 5–7cm larger than your pie dish. Lift the pastry over the rolling pin and lower it gently into the pie dish. Press the pastry firmly into the dish and up the sides, making sure there are no air bubbles. Put it in the fridge to chill while you prepare the filling.

Preheat the oven to 200°C/Fan 180°C/Gas 6. Place a baking tray in the oven to heat up.

For the filling, mix the sugar, cinnamon and cornflour in a large bowl, then stir in the apples and blackberries. Spoon the filling into the pie dish, making sure that it rises above the edge. Brush the rim of the dish with beaten egg.

Roll out the reserved ball of pastry. Cover the pie with the pastry and press the edges together firmly to seal them. Using a sharp knife, trim off the excess pastry, then gently crimp all around the edge. Make a few small holes in the centre of the pie with the tip of a knife. Glaze the top with beaten egg.

Lightly knead the pastry trimmings and re-roll. Cut the pastry into leaf shapes and decorate the pie as you desire, then brush with more beaten egg. Sprinkle the top of the pie with sugar. Place the pie on the baking tray and bake for 45–55 minutes or until the top is golden-brown and the filling is cooked.

Jam roly poly

You can't get any more British than a roly poly pudding, traditionally made in the well-washed sleeve of an old shirt! This is another favourite pud from when we were kids and it's a proper warming rib-sticker. It's made with simple store-cupboard ingredients and we think it tastes the business – especially with a good splash of custard.

Serves 6

softened butter, for
  greasing
200g self-raising flour,
  plus extra for dusting
100g shredded suet
1 tbsp caster sugar
good pinch of fine sea salt
150ml milk or water
6–7 tbsp raspberry or
  strawberry jam

Preheat the oven to 200°C/Fan 180°C/Gas 6. Cut a sheet of baking paper, about 38 x 38cm square, butter it and set it aside. Place a low rack in a smallish roasting tin.

Put the flour, suet, sugar and salt in a large bowl and mix well. Slowly add the milk or water, stirring constantly until the mixture forms a soft, spongy dough. Turn the dough out on to a floured surface and knead it well, then roll it out to a rectangle measuring about 22 x 32cm.

Drop large spoonfuls of jam on to the dough, leaving a 1.5cm border all the way around the outside. Gently roll up the dough from one of the short ends and carefully transfer it to the baking paper, seam-side down. Wrap the roly poly in the baking paper, making a long pleat to allow the pudding to rise.

Twist the ends of the paper like a Christmas cracker to seal and tie each end tightly with kitchen string. Then put the roly poly on a large sheet of foil and wrap it up, again making a pleat and twisting the ends to seal. Place the pudding on the rack in the roasting tin and pour in just-boiled water around it. The water should not rise more than a centimetre up the sides of the pudding. Place the pudding in the oven and bake for about an hour.

Remove the tin and carefully lift the pudding off the rack. Unwrap the foil, then snip the string and unwrap the paper. The pudding should be well risen and lightly browned in places. Don't worry if some of the jam has made it's way through to the outside of the pudding – it will taste all the more delicious. Cut the roly poly into thick slices and serve with hot custard (see page 276) or cream.

Hairy Biker baked cheesecake

Everyone needs a good cheesecake recipe and this is one of our favourites. It's easy to make and delicious to eat, with a good splosh of booze and a crunchy coating. Amaretti are nice little almondy biscuits and you'll find them in the supermarket.

Serves 12

15g softened butter,
  for greasing
40g crunchy amaretti
  biscuits
750g ricotta cheese
150g caster sugar
6 eggs
100ml double cream
grated zest of 1 lemon
4 tbsp amaretto liqueur

Preheat the oven to 180°C/Fan 160°C/Gas 4. Grease the base and sides of a 24cm springform cake tin with butter. Put the base of the tin in upside down so that it will be easier to remove the cheesecake once it is ready.

Put the biscuits into a food processor and blitz them to fine crumbs. Alternatively, put them into a strong plastic bag and crush them with a rolling pin. Dust the crushed biscuits over the bottom and the sides of the cake tin, tilting and shaking to get an even coating. Keep back some of the crumbs to sprinkle on the top of the finished cheesecake.

Drain the ricotta cheese and put it in a mixing bowl with the sugar. Using an electric hand-held beater, whisk until well combined. Gradually add the eggs, one at a time, whisking well in between each addition.

Stir in the cream, lemon zest and the amaretto liqueur. The mixture should be very soft and light. Slowly pour the mixture into the prepared tin, starting in the middle to avoid disturbing the crumbs. Put the tin on a baking tray and bake the cheesecake for 10 minutes.

Turn the oven down to 160°C/Fan 140°C/Gas 3 and cook for a further hour, or until the cheesecake is just set. If the cheesecake does start to go brown on top while it is still very wobbly, cover it loosely with a large piece of foil.

When the cheesecake is ready, turn the oven off and open the door slightly. Wedge a folded tea towel or wooden spoon in the door to keep it ajar and leave the cheesecake to cool completely. This will take 3–4 hours and should prevent the top from cracking. When the cake is completely cool, put it in the fridge for at least 2 hours.

Slide a knife around the cheesecake, taking care to keep as much of the crumb as possible, and release it gently from the tin. Slide it off the tin base on to a serving plate and sprinkle the top with the reserved amaretti crumbs. Cut into wedges to serve.

Deep-fried ice cream with rum and raisin sauce

Phwoar – this is a real show-stopper, slam-dunk of a pud. It's everything naughty you can think of, all in one miraculous combo. We once suggested serving it at a banquet for 400 people but the team went on strike!

Serves 4–6

Ice cream

1 litre vanilla ice cream
150g gingernut biscuits
75g desiccated coconut
2 eggs, beaten
2 tbsp coconut cream
vegetable oil, for
    deep- frying

Rum and raisin sauce

150g raisins
150ml dark rum
1 tsp ground cinnamon
zest of 1 lime
200g granulated sugar
100ml double cream
pinch of salt

Place a small baking tray in the freezer for at least 20 minutes, until it's very cold. Remove it from the freezer. Use an ice-cream scoop to make balls of ice cream, each about the same size as a golf ball. Place them on the baking tray and freeze them for at least an hour, preferably longer.

In a food processor, blitz the biscuits to the texture of fine breadcrumbs, then mix them with the desiccated coconut. Mix the eggs in a separate bowl with the coconut cream.

Remove the ice cream from the freezer. Dip each ball into the biscuit and coconut mixture, patting it on to the ice cream. Then dip each ball into the egg and coconut cream mixture, then coat in the biscuit and coconut mixture again. Repeat this step again, to make sure you get a really thick crust with no risk of leakages. Put the coated balls back in the freezer, this time for several hours or preferably overnight.

Meanwhile, for the sauce, put the raisins and rum in a saucepan with the cinnamon. Bring to the boil, then immediately remove the pan from the heat and add the lime zest. Leave the mixture to infuse while you make the caramel for the sauce.

Put the sugar in a pan with 100ml of water. Stir until the sugar looks like very wet sand. Set the pan over a medium heat and leave it until the sugar starts to dissolve. Do not stir, but carefully shake the pan every so often if the caramel looks as though it is cooking unevenly. When it has turned an amber colour, remove the pan from the heat and pour in the cream – it will splutter and bubble, so be careful. If the caramel seizes up, set the pan over a low heat and stir until it has dissolved back into a sauce. Add the infused rum and raisins. Taste, season with salt and add more rum if needed.

When you are ready to fry the ice cream, heat the oil in a large pan or a deep-fat fryer to 190°C. Be careful. Hot oil can be dangerous so do not leave it unattended.

Remove the ice cream balls from the freezer at the last minute, and immediately lower them into the oil and cook for about 15 seconds, until they are a rich golden-brown colour. Drain on kitchen paper and serve at once with the rum and raisin sauce.

Upside-down banana tart

The French name for this is tarte tatin but we like to call our British Biker version how it is – upside down! These tarts can be made with all sorts of fruit but bananas go beautifully sticky and gooey – we were inspired by the toffee bananas we love in Chinese restaurants. Serve with custard and you'll be in pudding heaven.

Serves 6

200g caster sugar

150g butter, diced

pinch of ground cardamom (optional)

grated zest of 1 orange (optional)

4–5 bananas, peeled and cut into 2cm slices

375g puff pastry

Preheat the oven to 180°C/Fan 160°C/Gas 4.

Put the sugar in an ovenproof frying pan, about 23cm in diameter, and set it over a medium heat. Don't stir the sugar – just swirl it around once in a while, until it has melted and turned a light caramel colour. Remove the pan from the heat and add the butter. The liquid will bubble up, then subside, and you can then whisk in the butter. If the caramel splits, add a tablespoon of warm water and whisk – the sauce should emulsify again.

Sprinkle in the cardamom and orange zest, if using. Arrange the slices of banana over the caramel – they should be quite a snug fit.

Roll out the puff pastry and trim it into a round to fit your pan. Prick it lightly all over with a fork, then place it on top of the bananas, tucking in the edges as you go. Bake for 40–45 minutes, or until the pastry is a rich golden-brown. Allow to cool slightly.

To turn the tart out, place a plate over it and carefully turn the pan over to invert the tart on to the plate. Wear oven gloves to protect your hands, as the pan handle and the caramel will still be very hot. Cut into slices and serve with custard.

Bread and butter pudding with orange and raspberries

We think this is one of the all-time great British puds. We're pretty proud of this version, which is quite glam, made with slices of brioche and flavoured with orange zest, raspberries and a splash of raspberry liqueur if you have some in the cupboard. It's really easy to make too and you're gonna love it!

Serves 6

———

softened butter

10–12 slices of a
   square brioche loaf

300g raspberries

1–2 tbsp Framboise
   liqueur (optional)

125g caster sugar

4 eggs

400ml whole milk

400ml double cream

grated zest of 1
   large orange

1–2 tbsp demerara sugar

Butter a shallow ovenproof pudding dish. Butter the brioche slices and cut them in half on the diagonal. Arrange a layer of slices, buttered-side up, in the dish.

Put 100g of the raspberries in a bowl and sprinkle them with the Framboise, if using, and 2 tablespoons of the caster sugar. Crush the berries lightly, then spoon them over the brioche layer. Sprinkle over a few more whole raspberries. Top with the remaining brioche slices, then arrange the remaining raspberries over the brioche – tuck a few in between the slices as well as leaving a fair few on top.

Whisk the remaining sugar with the eggs, then add the milk, double cream and orange zest. Make sure everything is well combined, then pour this mixture over the brioche and raspberries. Leave the pudding to stand for about half an hour. Preheat the oven to 180°C/Fan 160°C/Gas 4.

Dot the pudding with a few knobs of butter, then sprinkle over the demerara sugar. Bake it in the oven for 35–45 minutes, until it is well set and the bread is golden-brown and lightly toasted in places. Lovely hot or cold.

Sticky toffee pudding

There's nothing better than a bowlful of this greatest of Cumbrian classics on a rainy winter Sunday. It warms you up and cheers you up. And it's a great recipe for when you're entertaining friends and family, as you can get it all prepared in advance, then heat it through when you're ready to eat.

Serves 6–8

50g butter, plus extra
   for greasing
200g pitted dates,
   roughly chopped
1 tsp bicarbonate of soda
300ml just-boiled water
75g light soft brown sugar
75g dark muscovado sugar
2 eggs
175g self-raising flour

Sauce
125g butter
75g light soft brown sugar
50g dark muscovado sugar
200ml double or
   whipping cream
pinch of salt

Preheat the oven to 180°C/Fan 160°C/Gas 4. Butter an ovenproof dish – either a large traditional oval one or a brownie tin measuring about 20 x 30cm.

Put the dates and bicarb in a bowl and cover them with the just-boiled water, then leave to stand. Put the 50g of butter and the sugars in a bowl and beat with an electric beater until very soft and fluffy. Add the eggs, one a time, adding a heaped tablespoon of flour with each addition. Fold in the rest of the flour. Add the dates and their soaking water and stir briefly to combine, then pour the mixture into the prepared dish. Bake the pudding in the oven for 25–30 minutes until it is springy to the touch and slightly shrinking away from the sides.

While the pudding is baking, make the sauce. Put all the ingredients in a pan, place over a low heat and stir until the butter has melted and the sugars have dissolved. Turn up the heat and bring the sauce to the boil, then simmer for a few minutes, until the sauce has thickened to the consistency of a light custard – it should coat the back of a spoon.

While the pudding is still hot, poke holes over the surface and pour over half the sauce. Leave the pudding to stand for a while – if you like, you can leave it for a couple of days and it will just get stickier. When you're ready to eat, warm it through again and serve with the rest of the sauce, also warmed through. Serve with cream or ice cream.

Rice pudding with prunes

You can't get any more British than a rice pud, but it doesn't have to be cooked in the oven for ages. This version is cooked on the hob, more like a risotto, and is totally great. We like to serve it with the prune compote and if you're completely decadent – some double cream! The prunes can be made in advance if you like.

Serves 6

———

150g pudding rice
1.25 litres whole milk
1 cinnamon stick
½ whole nutmeg
50g golden caster sugar
25g cut mixed peel
20g flaked almonds
pinch of sea salt

Prune compote
150ml Marsala wine
1 tbsp brandy
juice and zest of 1 orange
25g golden caster sugar
150g no-soak dried prunes

To prepare the prunes, gently heat the Marsala, brandy, orange juice and sugar in a small saucepan and stir until the sugar dissolves. Add the prunes and orange zest and bring to a gentle simmer.

Cook for 5 minutes, or until the liquid has reduced by half, stirring occasionally. Remove the pan from the heat and leave to stand while you prepare the rice.

For the rice pudding, put the rice, 1 litre of the milk and the cinnamon stick in a large pan and finely grate the nutmeg over the top. Stir and bring to a very gentle simmer. Cook for 20 minutes, stirring very regularly until the rice is looking thick and creamy.

Stir in the sugar, the rest of the milk and the mixed peel. Bring back to a gentle simmer and cook for another 35–40 minutes, or until the rice is very tender and creamy. Make sure you stir it well towards the end of the cooking time as the rice thickens. Taste the rice and if it is still a little hard or chalky in the middle, continue cooking for 5–10 minutes more, adding a little more milk or water if necessary.

While the rice is cooking, toast the almonds in a dry pan over a low heat until they're lightly browned, turning them occasionally.

Remove the cinnamon stick and stir a pinch of salt into the rice. Serve with the prunes and scatter the toasted almonds on top.

Rhubarb and custard tart

Rhubarb and custard is one of the all-time classic partnerships and here they are combined in a tart to be proud of. Yes, there is a bit of work to do but it can all be done in advance and it's well worth it we promise.

Serves 8

3 medium eggs

2 medium egg yolks

100g caster sugar

300ml whole milk

300ml double cream, plus extra to pour

1 vanilla pod, split lengthways

Rhubarb topping

65g caster sugar, plus extra to taste

400–500g rhubarb (preferably forced rhubarb), trimmed

Pastry

250g plain flour, plus extra for dusting

150g cold butter, cut into cubes

1 egg, beaten with 1 tbsp cold water

You need a deep 23cm loose-bottomed tart tin that's about 4cm deep.

To make the pastry, put the flour and butter into a food processor and pulse until the mixture resembles fine breadcrumbs. Gradually add the beaten egg and mix until the mixture forms a rough ball.

Tip the pastry on to a floured surface and roll it out into a circle roughly 5cm larger than the tart tin and about the thickness of a pound coin. Turn the pastry 90 degrees every couple of rolls to create an even thickness.

Lift the pastry over the rolling pin and lower it gently into the flan tin. Push the pastry into the base and sides of the tin. Trim the pastry by pinching it between your thumb and finger, lifting it slightly above the rim of the tin. Roll the trimmings into a ball and wrap them in cling film to use for patching the cooked tart if necessary. Prick the base lightly with a fork and chill in the fridge for 30 minutes.

Preheat the oven to 200°C/Fan 180°C/Gas 6. Place the chilled pastry case on a baking tray. Line the inside with crumpled baking paper and half-fill with baking beans or dried beans.

Bake for 25 minutes, then carefully take it out of the oven and remove the paper and beans. Put the pastry case back in the oven for a further 3 minutes, or until the surface of the pastry is dry.

Remove the pastry case from the oven and reduce the temperature to 160°C/Fan 140°C/Gas 3. If the pastry has any holes, patch them with the reserved pastry to stop any of the filling leaking out.

For the filling, whisk the eggs, egg yolks and sugar in a heatproof bowl with a metal whisk until smooth. Set aside.

Put the milk and cream into a medium pan. Stir the split vanilla pod and seeds into the milk and cream. Heat the liquid gently until it's hot but not boiling, stirring regularly, then remove the vanilla pod. Slowly stir the milk and cream into the bowl of egg mixture until thoroughly combined. Pour the custard into the prepared pastry case.

Bake the custard in the oven for 40–45 minutes, or until it is only just set. It should still be fairly wobbly in the middle, as it will continue to set as it cools. Remove the tin from the oven and leave the tart to cool completely. Put it in the fridge to chill for at least 2 hours.

For the rhubarb topping, place the sugar and a tablespoon of water in a large non-stick frying pan over a low heat. Stir until the sugar is dissolved. Add the rhubarb to the pan in a single layer. Cook it gently for 4 minutes, then turn it over and cook on the other side for a further 3–4 minutes, or until softened but not falling apart.

Remove the rhubarb from the pan and tip it into a large bowl. Add a little extra sugar, to taste, if needed, and leave it to cool. Chill in the fridge until needed.

Just before serving, slowly release the tart from the tin. Transfer it to a serving plate or board. Spoon the rhubarb on top of the tart and serve immediately, with some extra cream if you like.

Plum pavlova

British plums are the best so make good use of them in the autumn and whip up this truly awesome pavlova. This meringue marvel is a gift from our friends down under and a pleasure to behold.

Serves 8

————

5 egg whites
1 tsp ground cinnamon
250g caster sugar
1 tsp white wine vinegar

Cherries
100g dried cherries
100ml kirsch

Spiced plums
200ml red wine
juice of 1 orange
75g light brown sugar
1 cinnamon stick
a few cardamom pods,
   lightly crushed
a few allspice berries,
   lightly crushed
1 strip of thinly
   pared orange zest
8 ripe plums, stoned
   and quartered

To assemble
300ml double or
   whipping cream
1 tbsp icing sugar
½ tsp cinnamon (optional)

First make the meringue. Preheat the oven to 150°C/Fan 130°C/Gas 2. Draw a circle of about 23cm in diameter on a sheet of baking paper and place this on a baking tray.

Beat the egg whites with a hand-held electric whisk, until soft peaks form when the whisk is removed from the bowl.

Mix the cinnamon with the sugar, then slowly add this to the egg whites. Add a tablespoon at a time to start with and then slightly more, beating in between each addition, until the meringue is stiff and glossy. Sprinkle over the vinegar and fold it in.

Use a few blobs of the meringue to secure the baking paper to the baking tray, then pile the rest into the marked circle. Make a slight indentation in the middle and allow the meringue to form peaks around the side.

Bake the meringue in the oven for about an hour and 15 minutes, to an hour and a half. It should be crisp round the sides but with some give in the middle. Turn off the oven and leave the meringue in there to cool completely.

To prepare the cherries, put them in a small saucepan with the kirsch. Bring to the boil, then turn the heat down and simmer until the cherries are soft and plump and most of the kirsch has been absorbed.

To make the spiced plums, put the wine, orange juice, sugar, spices and orange zest in a saucepan and stir over a low heat until the sugar has dissolved. Bring to the boil and simmer for a few minutes until the mixture is syrupy. Add the plums and poach them in the liquid for a few minutes, or until soft but still holding their shape.

Remove the plums from the liquid, peeling off the skins as you go – they should just fall off. Strain the cooking liquid.

To assemble, whip the cream and add the icing sugar and the cinnamon, if using, then stir in a couple of tablespoons of the plum liquid and the cherries. Spoon the cream over the meringue base, top with the plums and drizzle over any remaining liquid.

Chocolate fondants

The chocoholics' favourite, these little puddings should be gloriously gooey on the inside, oozing melted choc. They're not difficult to make but you do need to get the timing right. A real top turn.

Serves 6

150g butter, plus extra
    for greasing

1 tsp cocoa powder

1 tsp plain flour

150g plain chocolate,
    (minimum 70%
    cocoa solids), broken
    into pieces

3 large eggs

3 large egg yolks

50g caster sugar

finely grated zest of
    2 limes

25g self-raising flour

crème fraiche, clotted
    cream or ice cream,
    to serve

Generously grease 6 x 175ml dariole moulds with butter, then line the base of each with a small circle of baking paper.

Mix the cocoa powder and plain flour in a bowl and sift a little into each dariole mould, rolling them around to coat the base and sides. Shake out any excess.

Bring some water to a simmer in a saucepan. Place a heatproof bowl over the water, making sure the bottom of the bowl doesn't touch the water. Add the chocolate and butter to the bowl and stir until melted and smooth. Remove the bowl from the pan and set aside to cool for 10 minutes.

Meanwhile, whisk the eggs, egg yolks, caster sugar and half the lime zest together in a bowl, using an electric whisk. When the mixture is pale and thick, and the whisk leaves a trail across the mixture when lifted out, the mixture is ready.

Gently fold in the cooled, melted chocolate mixture using a large, metal spoon, until just combined. Sift in the self-raising flour and fold in until just combined.

Pour the fondant mixture into the prepared moulds, cover them with cling film and chill in the fridge for at least 30 minutes and up to 8 hours.

To cook the fondants, preheat the oven to 200°C/Fan 180°C/Gas 6. Remove the fondants from the fridge and allow them to come up to room temperature. Take off the cling film and place the moulds on a baking tray.

Bake for 11 minutes, or until the sponge has risen but the puddings still have a slight wobble. Remove them from the oven.

Using a folded, dry tea towel or oven glove to protect your hand, loosen the chocolate fondant from the sides of each dariole mould using a blunt, round-edged knife and turn them out on to plates. Remove the circles of baking paper and top the fondants with spoonfuls of crème fraiche, clotted cream or ice cream, if using. Sprinkle with the rest of the lime zest and serve immediately.

Treacle pudding

This is a proper old-fashioned steamed pudding. Treacle pud is a British classic but we've always been big fans of banana in desserts so we've added some to the traditional recipe to make it even more delicious. Don't worry if the sponge turns a bit purple – it's just the potassium in the bananas and it's good for you. *Dave*: I love bananas because they've got no bones!

Serves 6

175g softened butter,
  plus extra for greasing

2 tbsp golden syrup

2 large bananas (1 sliced
  on the diagonal and
  1 mashed)

175g soft light brown
  sugar

3 eggs

175g self-raising flour

squeeze of lime juice

Butter the insides of a large pudding basin thoroughly. Put the golden syrup in the base, then arrange the sliced banana over it.

Using an electric whisk, mix the butter and sugar together until light, fluffy and creamy. Add the eggs one at a time with a tablespoon of flour after each one, then mix in the rest of the flour and the mashed banana. Add a squeeze of lime juice to loosen the consistency slightly, then scrape the mixture into the pudding basin.

Cover the basin with a sheet of greaseproof paper, or foil, with a pleat folded down the middle – this allows the pudding to expand during cooking. Put an upturned heatproof saucer or a folded tea towel in a large, deep pan and place the pudding basin on top. Add enough just-boiled water to the pan to come halfway up the sides of the basin. Cover the pan with a tight-fitting lid and place over a low heat. Leave the pudding to steam in the gently simmering water for 2 hours. Make sure the pan does not boil dry and add more boiling water when necessary. The pudding is done when a skewer inserted into the centre of the pudding (through the paper or foil) comes out clean.

When the pudding is ready, turn off the heat and carefully lift the basin from the water. Leave it to stand for 5 minutes.

Discard the paper or foil. Run a round-bladed knife around the edge of the pudding to loosen the sides. Carefully turn the pudding out on to a deep plate and remove the basin. Serve with some custard.

Apple crumble

No one ever grumbles about a crumble. It's a really quick and easy pudding to make and you can use all sorts of fruit – although apple is the classic and our personal favourite. We've added almonds to the topping for some extra crunch and flavour.

Serves 6

4 eating apples, peeled, quartered and cored

2 Bramley cooking apples, peeled, quartered and cored

100g demerara sugar

2 tsp cinnamon

Topping

150g plain flour

100g golden caster sugar

100g butter, cut into cubes

50g flaked almonds

Preheat the oven to 200°C/Fan 180°C/Gas 6. Put all the apples in an ovenproof dish, add the sugar and cinnamon and mix well.

To make the topping, mix the flour and caster sugar in a bowl, then add the butter and rub it into the dry ingredients with your fingertips. The mixture should have the texture of coarse breadcrumbs. Add the flaked almonds and mix well.

Sprinkle the topping over the apples and bake the crumble in the preheated oven for about 30 minutes or until the top is golden brown and the apples are cooked.

Serve with cream or custard.

Hairy Biker tip: You can add 50g of oats to the crumble mixture for a bit of extra chewiness.

Lemon meringue pie

Si: my mam's pie was absolutely the best. *Dave*: my mother's lemon meringue pie came in a box, but now I know better. This recipe is lemony perfection.

Serves 6

50g cornflour
350ml cold water
200g caster sugar
zest and juice of 4 lemons
3 eggs yolks
1 whole egg

Meringue topping
3 eggs whites
175g caster sugar
½ tsp vanilla extract

Pastry
200g plain flour,
    plus extra for dusting
1 tsp caster sugar
125g cold butter,
    cut into cubes
1 egg, beaten

Preheat the oven to 200°C/Fan 180°C/Gas 6. Grease a 20cm flan tin.

To make the pastry, place the flour, sugar and the butter in a food processor and pulse until the mixture resembles fine breadcrumbs. With the motor running, gradually add the beaten egg and blend until the mixture forms a ball. Don't overwork the pastry or it will be tough.

Tip the pastry on to a floured board, knead briefly, then roll it out to the thickness of a pound coin, turning the pastry and flouring the surface regularly. Use the pastry to line the prepared tin. Trim the edges neatly, prick the base lightly with a fork and chill the pastry in the fridge for 30 minutes.

To make the filling, put the cornflour in a small bowl and mix with enough of the water to make a thin paste, then set aside. Pour the remaining water into a pan and add the sugar, lemon zest and juice. You should have about 225ml lemon juice. Heat gently until the sugar dissolves then bring to the boil. Reduce the heat slightly and quickly stir in the cornflour mixture – the sauce should thicken immediately.

Cook over a low heat for 3 minutes, stirring until thickened and glossy. Remove from the heat and cool for 5 minutes. Whisk the egg yolks with the whole egg until smooth, then whisk vigorously into the sauce. Set aside to cool for 25 minutes.

Put the pastry case on a baking tray, line with crumpled baking paper and fill with baking beans. Bake the pastry blind for 15 minutes then take it out of the oven and remove the paper and beans. Return to the oven for a further 3–4 minutes until the surface of the pastry is dry. Remove from the oven and reduce the temperature to 150°C/Fan 130°C/Gas 2.

For the meringue topping, whisk the egg whites in a large bowl until stiff, then gradually whisk in half the sugar. Add the vanilla extract and whisk in the remaining sugar.

Stir the cooled lemon filling and pour into the pastry case. Cover very gently with large dessert spoonfuls of the meringue topping, starting at the sides then working your way into the middle, and gently swirl the top. Bake for 25 minutes or until the meringue is set and very lightly browned. Leave to cool before removing from the tin.

Raspberry fool with almond biscuits

Fruit fools are a classic British dessert that date back to the 16th century – but no one seems to know quite how they got the name. All we can say is that you'd be a fool not to try this recipe.

Serves 4

200g frozen raspberries

300ml double cream

50g icing sugar

½ tsp rosewater (optional)

2 tbsp flaked almonds, toasted (optional), to serve

Almond thins

100g butter, softened

100g light soft brown sugar

a few drops of almond extract

100g ground almonds

100g plain flour

pinch of salt

To make the biscuits, preheat the oven to 180°C/Fan 160°C/Gas 4. Beat the butter and sugar together in a bowl until very light, soft and fluffy, then beat in the almond extract. Mix the ground almonds and flour together with a pinch of salt, then fold this mixture into the butter and sugar.

Bring everything together into a soft dough, then form into 24 balls. Arrange these over 2 baking trays. Bake the biscuits in the preheated oven for 10–12 minutes until they are starting to colour around the edges, then remove. Leave them to cool and firm up on the baking tray. They keep well in an airtight container for several days.

To make the fool, lightly crush the raspberries while they are still frozen. Whisk the cream and sugar together until they form peaks – you don't want the mixture too stiff so don't overwhisk. Stir in the rosewater, if using.

Divide half the cream mixture between 4 glasses, followed by the frozen raspberries. Top with the remaining cream. Very gently stir the contents of each glass until you have a ripple effect. Wipe around the edges at the top, then cover and chill. Sprinkle with the almonds just before serving, if using.

FAB FESTIVE FEASTS

Nut roast with mushroom gravy

Not everyone wants meat for a festive feast and this nut roast is just right for a celebration at any time of year. It freezes well too, so great to have as a standby for when you want to show your veggie mates you love them.

Serves 8–10

300g spinach

50g dried cranberries

50ml oloroso sherry

1 tbsp olive oil

15g butter

1 onion, finely chopped

200g chestnut mushrooms, finely chopped

1 large parsnip, coarsely grated (about 250g)

2 garlic cloves, chopped

1 tsp dried sage

1 thyme sprig

zest of 1 lemon

150g cooked freekah or spelt grains

100g mixed nuts, chopped

100g cooked chestnuts, crumbled

25g fresh breadcrumbs

3 eggs, beaten

25g butter

sea salt and black pepper

Gravy

1 tbsp olive oil

15g butter

1 shallot, chopped

250g chestnut mushrooms, finely chopped

1 garlic clove, chopped

a few thyme leaves

100ml oloroso sherry

250ml vegetable stock

50ml single cream

Wash the spinach in plenty of water and put it in a saucepan. Heat gently until it has wilted down, stirring a couple of times, then drain it well in a sieve. Leave to cool, then chop it roughly.

Put the cranberries into a small saucepan and cover them with the sherry. Bring to the boil, remove the pan from the heat and set aside until the cranberries have plumped up and absorbed most of the sherry.

Heat the olive oil and butter in a frying pan. Add the onion and mushrooms and cook them over a medium heat until any liquid coming out of the mushrooms has evaporated and the onion has softened. Add the parsnip and continue to cook until the parsnip has reduced in volume and the onion has started to caramelise. Add the garlic, dried sage, thyme and lemon zest, then cook for a couple more minutes. Remove the pan from the heat and allow the mixture to cool slightly.

Preheat the oven to 200°C/Fan 180°C/Gas 6. Line a 900g loaf tin with some baking paper.

Put the freekah or spelt into a large bowl along with the mixed nuts, chestnuts, breadcrumbs, spinach, cooked vegetables and the eggs. Season well with salt and pepper and mix thoroughly.

Spoon the mixture into the lined loaf tin and dot the butter over the top. Smooth the mixture down, but don't pack it too tightly. Cover with a layer of greaseproof paper and bake in the oven for about an hour or until piping hot.

Meanwhile, to make the gravy, heat the olive oil and butter in a pan. Add the shallot and cook for several minutes until it's starting to caramelise around the edges. Add the mushrooms and cook them for 5 minutes, stirring regularly. Add the garlic and thyme, season well and continue to cook for a couple of minutes. Turn up the heat and pour in the sherry. Allow it to bubble until almost completely evaporated, then add the stock. Simmer, covered, for 10 minutes. Stir in the cream just before serving.

Slice the nut roast and serve it with the gravy and cranberry sauce (see page 273).

Stilton-stuffed figs with apple and beetroot sauce

Christmas isn't Christmas without some Stilton – that classic British blue cheese. These tasty figs, stuffed with cheese and wrapped in ham, make a perfect nibble or starter for any festive feast. Choose figs that aren't too ripe so they don't collapse when in the oven.

Serves 8

—————

8 medium to large figs
40–50g Stilton cheese
8 slices of Parma ham
2 tsp honey
1 tsp olive oil
a few thyme leaves
sea salt and black pepper

Apple and beetroot sauce

200g cooked beetroot, finely diced
1 eating apple, grated
½ small red onion, very finely chopped
a few thyme leaves
a few tarragon leaves, very finely chopped
2 tbsp walnut oil
1 tbsp cider vinegar
25g walnuts, chopped

Preheat the oven to 200°C/Fan 180°C/Gas 6. Trim the top stem of each fig if necessary, then cut a cross almost to the base. Squeeze the figs from the base so the tips splay outwards.

Mash up the Stilton cheese, then stuff about a teaspoon into the centre of each fig. Wrap the figs in the Parma ham – the ham should come about two-thirds up the fig, leaving the tips and the cheese exposed.

Place the stuffed figs in a small baking dish. Drizzle them with the honey and olive oil, then sprinkle over the thyme leaves and season with salt and pepper.

Bake the figs in the oven for 10–15 minutes, or until the cheese has melted and the ham has browned.

To make the sauce, put the beetroot, apple, onion and herbs in a bowl. Season well with salt and pepper. Whisk together the oil and vinegar and season with salt. Pour this dressing over the beetroot mixture and stir to combine. Sprinkle in the walnuts.

Serve the sauce with the stuffed figs.

Posh cheese balls

In France, these are known as 'gougères' but cheese balls does it for us. This recipe does make a lot but we can tell you – they disappear fast. The dough can be made several hours in advance or, if you really want to prepare ahead, the piped-out rounds can be open frozen, then cooked from frozen.

Makes 48

85g unsalted butter

1 tsp sea salt

150g plain flour, well sifted

1 tsp mustard powder

4 eggs

75g Gruyère
  cheese, grated

25g Parmesan
  cheese, grated

To sprinkle

1 tbsp grated
  Gruyère cheese,

1 tbsp grated
  Parmesan cheese

Filling (optional)

200g mascarpone

50ml double cream

up to 1 tbsp truffle oil
  or garlic oil (optional)

sea salt and black pepper

Preheat the oven to 200°C/Fan 180°C/Gas 6. Line 2 baking trays with baking paper. Fit a 1cm round nozzle on a piping bag.

Put the butter and salt into a pan with 250ml of water. Set the pan over a high heat and bring the water to the boil, stirring until the butter has melted. Add the sifted flour and mustard powder all at once, then whisk until the batter is smooth. Continue to cook for another minute or so – the mixture will come away from the sides and form a non-sticky ball. You may also see a thin layer coat the base of the pan. Remove the pan from the heat and leave the mixture to cool for 3–4 minutes.

Add the eggs, one at a time, to the cooled mixture and beat each one in thoroughly with a wooden spoon or whisk. Finally, stir in the grated cheese.

Put half the batter into the piping bag, and pipe 4cm diameter rounds on to the baking trays, spacing them out evenly – you should be able to fit about 12 on each tray. Wet a finger and smooth off any tips which may have appeared on the rounds. Mix the extra grated cheeses together and sprinkle half of it over the rounds. Put the trays in the oven and bake the cheese balls for 10 minutes until they are lightly coloured. Turn the heat down to 180°C/Fan 160°C/Gas 4 and continue to cook until the cheese balls are well puffed up and dry in the centre – they should sound hollow when tapped. This will take another 20–25 minutes. Don't undercook them as they will collapse as they cool.

Remove the trays from the oven and make a little hole in the side of each ball to help the steam escape. Repeat with the remaining batter and cheese, then bake as before. Serve the cheese balls straight from the oven, or leave to cool and reheat before serving.

If you want to fill the cheese balls, allow them to cool completely. Mix the mascarpone and double cream, then beat in the truffle oil or garlic oil, if using, a little at a time. Taste as you go until you are happy with the strength. Season with salt and pepper. Take a clean piping bag with smaller nozzle and spoon the mascarpone mixture into it, then pipe a small amount into each cheese ball.

Lobster mac 'n' cheese

Macaroni and cheese is a favourite British supper dish. In this recipe we've poshed it up with some lobster tails to serve as a festive treat for any occasion. Frozen lobster is fine.

Serves 4

300g macaroni

4 cooked lobster tails, shell on

100ml white wine

750ml milk

1 bay leaf

slice of onion

1 tbsp vegetable oil

50g butter

1 onion, finely diced

50g streaky bacon, cut into small pieces

2 garlic cloves, sliced

1 thyme sprig, leaves only

60g plain flour

1 tsp mustard powder

¼ tsp cayenne pepper

75g Cheddar cheese, grated

75g Gruyère cheese, grated

50g fresh breadcrumbs

sea salt

To garnish

knob of butter

2 cooked lobster tails

2 tbsp brandy

Preheat the oven to 200°C/Fan 180°C/Gas 6. Bring a large saucepan of water to the boil and salt it generously. Add the macaroni and cook for 8–10 minutes, or until just shy of al dente. Drain well.

Shell the lobster tails, then chop the flesh into bite-sized chunks and set it aside. Put the shells in a pan and place over a high heat. Pour in the white wine and allow it to bubble fiercely. Remove from the heat and strain, discarding the shells and reserving the wine.

Put the milk, bay leaf and onion slice into a pan and heat slowly, until the milk is just below boiling point. Remove the pan from the heat and set it aside so the milk can infuse with the bay leaf and onion.

Heat the oil and butter in a large pan. Add the diced onion and the bacon and fry until the onion is lightly caramelised and the bacon is crisp and brown.

Add the garlic and thyme, then stir in the flour, mustard powder and cayenne. Stir, then gradually add the infused milk, stirring until it is all incorporated and you have a béchamel sauce. Add 50g of each of the cheeses and the reserved wine, then stir over a low heat until the cheese has melted.

Mix the sauce with the macaroni and stir in the lobster meat. Tip everything into a large, shallow ovenproof dish or into individual dishes if you prefer.

Mix the breadcrumbs with the remaining cheese and sprinkle this over the macaroni. Bake in the oven for 30–35 minutes, or until piping hot, browned and bubbling.

To garnish, heat a frying pan over a high heat. When it's hot add the butter and the lobster tails. Cook for 1 minute on each side until warmed through. Add the brandy and light with a match to flambé. Be careful – keep well back from the flames and allow to die down before serving. Remove the lobster tails from the pan, cut them in half lengthwise and place them on top of the macaroni cheese. Serve at once.

Glazed ham

A beautiful ham was a Christmas essential in both our houses when we were growing up and we think it's ideal for a feast at any time of year. The luscious bourbon and cherry glaze is what makes this recipe really stand out from the crowd.

Serves 8

2.5–3kg gammon joint, smoked or unsmoked, rolled and tied

1 large onion

6 cloves

4 bay leaves

1 thyme sprig

few allspice berries

2 carrots, peeled and roughly chopped

2 celery sticks, roughly chopped

a few peppercorns

Glaze

cloves, for studding

150g cherry conserve

100ml bourbon whiskey

20g fresh root ginger, finely grated

1 tbsp light soft brown sugar

½ tsp ground cinnamon

Put the gammon in a large saucepan and cover it with water. Bring to the boil, then drain. Rinse off any white starch from both the ham and the saucepan, then put the ham back in the pan and cover with fresh water.

Stud the onion with the cloves, and add this to the pan with the herbs, spices, carrots, celery and peppercorns.

Bring to the boil, then reduce the heat and leave the ham to simmer, covered, for 2–2½ hours, or until it is cooked through. The internal temperature should reach 68°C – use a meat thermometer to check if you have one. Remove the pan from the heat and either leave the ham to cool in the liquor or immediately transfer it to a work surface.

Preheat the oven to 200°C/Fan 180°C Fan/Gas 6.

To prepare the gammon for glazing, cut off the string and cut away the outer rind, leaving at least half the thickness of fat underneath attached to the ham. Score a diamond pattern on the fat and stud cloves into each corner.

To make the glaze, blend the cherry conserve – use a food processor or hand-held blender to get it as smooth as possible. Put the jam in a pan with the bourbon, ginger, sugar and cinnamon.

Bring to the boil and simmer for 15 minutes, or until the liquid has reduced enough to coat the back of a spoon. Brush the glaze over the ham, making sure you use it all.

Place the ham in a roasting tin and roast in the oven for 20–25 minutes, or until it is well browned. Carve into slices to serve.

Stuffed roast pork

Known as porchetta in Italy, this pork dish has become a much-loved classic in Britain and a great alternative to turkey for a festive meal. Boning, butterflying and stuffing the pork like this means that the flavours go all through the meat, especially if you leave it to marinate in the fridge for a couple of days. A crackling good dish!

Serves 6

3kg piece of boned belly pork attached to the loin, butterflied and rind scored

1.5kg potatoes, such as Maris Pipers, thickly sliced

1 onion, thickly sliced

100ml white wine or cider

100ml chicken stock or water

sea salt and black pepper

Filling

3 tbsp finely chopped rosemary

1 thyme sprig, leaves only, finely chopped

1 garlic bulb, cloves peeled and crushed

1 tbsp fennel seeds, crushed

1 tsp chilli flakes

zest of 1 lemon

50ml wine

For the filling, either put all the ingredients in a small food processor and blend until well combined – the mixture doesn't have to be completely smooth – or pound with a pestle and mortar. Season with salt and pepper.

Lay the pork out, skin-side down, and rub the filling over the meat. Roll it up as tightly as you can and secure at intervals with butcher's string.

If you have time, leave the pork in the fridge, uncovered or loosely wrapped in kitchen paper, overnight – or even better, for 2 nights. This gives the flavours time to permeate the meat and allows the skin to dry out.

An hour before you are ready to start cooking the pork, remove it from the fridge so it can come up to room temperature. Preheat the oven to 150°C/Fan 130°C/Gas 2.

Arrange the potatoes and onion slices on the base of a large roasting tin and season with salt. Pour over the white wine or cider and the stock or water.

Make sure the rind of the pork is dry and season it with salt. Place the pork on top of the potatoes and onions. Cover it with foil and put in the oven. Roast for 4 hours until the pork is cooked through. Check with a meat thermometer if you have one – the internal temperature should read 68°C.

Turn the oven up to its highest setting and cook for a further half an hour to crisp up the skin. Remove from the oven and transfer the meat and potatoes to separate serving dishes. Leave the meat to rest for half an hour, uncovered, but keep the potatoes warm.

Roast turkey and stuffing

Buy the best turkey you can afford, the more free-range the better. If you're only having a small gathering you might prefer a turkey crown, so we'll tell you how to cook that too at the end of this turkey recipe.

Serves 8–10

6kg oven-ready turkey,
    preferably with giblets
100g softened butter
sea salt and black pepper

Stuffing

600g sausage meat
1 turkey liver, finely
    chopped (if you
    have the giblets)
1 onion, finely chopped
200g chestnuts,
    peeled and roughly
    chopped (vacuum-
    packed are fine)
2 eating apples or quinces,
    cored and grated
1 tsp allspice berries,
    ground
1 tbsp fresh thyme leaves
4 tbsp finely chopped
    parsley
zest of 1 lemon

Gravy

turkey giblets
1 onion, roughly chopped
2 carrots, roughly chopped
2 celery sticks,
    roughly chopped
2 bay leaves
1 thyme sprig
500ml chicken stock
2 tbsp plain flour
100ml red or white wine

Put all the stuffing ingredients into a bowl and mix them thoroughly. This is best done by hand, rather than with a spoon. Make sure the mixture is at room temperature before stuffing the turkey. Preheat the oven to 190°C/Fan 170°C/Gas 5.

Weigh both the turkey and the stuffing, and calculate the cooking time from their combined weight. Split the stuffing between the cavity of the turkey and the neck end. At the neck, pull the skin up away from the flesh and place the stuffing between flesh and skin. Pull the neck flap down over the stuffing and tuck it under the bird.

Put the turkey, breast-side up, in a large roasting tin. Smear the butter all over it, concentrating on the breast, then season with salt and pepper. Take a large sheet of foil and use it to cover the whole bird, tucking it over the edges of the roasting tin.

To work out the cooking time, allow 20 minutes per kilo of bird and stuffing, plus a further 90 minutes. A 6kg turkey with stuffing will need about 3½ hours. Roast the turkey according to your calculations, then 50 minutes before the cooking time is up, remove the foil and continue to roast, allowing the skin to brown. Start checking to see if the turkey is done after 20 minutes.

The best way to check whether the turkey is cooked is to use a meat thermometer. The temperature of the thickest part of the meat – usually the thigh – should be 71°C. You can also pierce the same part of the thigh with a skewer and see if the juices run clear – if there's a hint of pinkness you need to cook it for longer.

To ensure the stuffing is properly cooked, insert a metal skewer into the cavity for 5 seconds. Take the skewer out, place it on your finger and if after 1 second it's too hot to touch, the stuffing is ready. When the turkey is done, transfer it to a large serving platter and cover with foil to rest while you make the gravy.

To make the gravy, first make the giblet stock while the turkey is roasting. Put the giblets, except the liver, in a pan with the onion, carrots, celery, bay leaves and thyme. Cover with 500ml of water and the stock, then season with salt and pepper. Bring to the boil, turn the heat down and simmer for 1–1½ hours. Strain the liquid through a sieve.

Strain the juices from the turkey roasting tin and spoon off as much fat as possible. Put the tin over a medium heat, pour the juices back in and sprinkle in the flour. Stir until thoroughly combined, scraping the sediment from the bottom of the tin. Add up to 500ml of giblet stock and stir until all the sediment is incorporated. Transfer the liquid to a saucepan and stir in the wine, then bring to a simmer and cook for a few minutes. Check for seasoning and add salt and pepper to taste.

Serve the turkey with the gravy, stuffing, cranberry sauce (see page 273), roast potatoes (see page 269) and whatever other veg you fancy.

Turkey crown

You can buy these easily, but you can also buy a whole turkey and save the legs for another time. Making the crown is a very simple process. Remove both the legs by cutting down between leg and breast until you get to the joint, push it down until it pops out, then cut through where it's still attached to the body. This will give you a full crown with the carcass still attached for the stuffing.

To cook, stuff the cavity and then weigh the bird. Preheat the oven to its highest setting and roast for half an hour. Turn the oven down to 180°C/Fan 160°C/Gas 4 and cook for another 15 minutes per kilo. Pierce the thickest part of the turkey with a skewer – when the juices run clear it's cooked. Make sure the stuffing is cooked as in the method for the whole turkey on the previous page.

Si's tip: You can use the turkey carcass to make stock, turkey curry or soup – leftover heaven.

Dave's tip: We recommend bronze turkeys. The name isn't anything to do with their ability in the Olympics – it's a type of turkey that tastes gamey and fabulous!

Mincemeat lattice tart

We love a mince pie but we think this lattice tart is even better – the surprise disc of marzipan inside makes it that bit special. It's based on an Austrian favourite called linzer torte and this is our version. Use a metal tart tin, rather than a ceramic one, and heat up a baking tray to put it on so the underside cooks well.

Serves 6–8

200g marzipan
500g mincemeat
milk, for brushing

Pastry
150g plain flour, plus
    extra for dusting
150g ground almonds
150g caster sugar
150g chilled butter,
    cut into cubes
1 egg, beaten

First make the pastry. Put the flour, almonds, caster sugar and butter in a food processor and whizz until the mixture resembles fine breadcrumbs. Add a pinch of salt and the egg and process again until it forms a ball of dough. Remove the dough from the processor – it will be very soft – and wrap it in cling film. Chill well.

Preheat the oven to 180°C/Fan 160°C/Gas 4 and put a baking tray in the oven to heat up.

Remove the pastry from the fridge and divide it into one-third and two-thirds. Dust your work surface with flour and roll out the larger piece of pastry to line a 25cm flan tin. Dust your work surface with more flour and roll out the marzipan into a round that will fit inside the pastry. Cover the marzipan with the mincemeat.

Roll out the remaining pastry and cut it into strips. Use it to make a lattice design on top of the mincemeat. Or if you like, cut out different shapes such as stars and use them to cover most of the mincemeat. Brush the pastry with milk.

Place the tart on the baking tray in the oven and bake for about 30 minutes, or until the pastry is crisp and golden-brown. Dust the tart with icing sugar and serve hot or cold, with some cream.

Last-minute Christmas cake

Traditionally, a Christmas cake has to be made weeks ahead of the big day to allow time to mature, but our latest version can be made at the last minute – phew! You will need a deep 20cm round tin or a 18cm square tin.

Serves 12

100g pre-soaked apricots
100g dried pineapple
100g candied peel
125g raisins
125g sultanas
100g currants
200g glacé cherries, halved
100g cashew nuts, chopped
zest of 1 lime, 1 lemon and ½ orange
200ml white port or rum
225g butter
225g golden caster sugar
175g plain flour
50g ground almonds
1 tsp ground cinnamon
1 tsp ground cardamom
½ tsp grated nutmeg
½ tsp ground allspice
¼ tsp ground cloves
pinch of salt
4 eggs
juice of ½ orange
1 tbsp rosewater

Decoration

500g marzipan
600g fondant icing
1 orange
icing sugar
3 tbsp apricot jam
3 or 4 rosemary sprigs
2 egg whites

Chop the apricots, pineapple and candied peel. Put them in a large bowl with the rest of the fruit and add the cashew nuts and citrus zest. Pour over the white port or rum, then leave to stand overnight, or at least for a few hours. When you are ready to make the cake, line a deep 20cm round tin or a 18cm square tin with baking paper. Tie a double layer of baking paper around the outside of the tin, making sure it is at least 10cm higher than the top of the tin. Preheat the oven to 170°C/Fan 150°C/Gas 3½.

Cream the butter and sugar in a large bowl until very pale, aerated and fluffy Put the flour, ground almonds and spices in a separate bowl together with a pinch of salt, and mix lightly to get rid of any lumps.

Add the eggs, one at a time, to the butter and sugar, and sprinkle over a tablespoon of the dry ingredients. Mix in, then repeat with the remaining eggs, adding a tablespoon of the flour mixture after each one. Add the rest of the flour and stir it in thoroughly. Add the reserved soaked fruit and the rosewater, then mix thoroughly. Scrape the mixture into the prepared tin and smooth over with a palette knife.

Bake the cake in the oven for 1 hour, then turn the temperature down to 150°C/ Fan130°C Fan/Gas 2, then bake for a further 2 hours. To check the cake is done, insert a skewer into the centre – it should come out clean. Leave the cake to cool in the tin for about 10 minutes, then put it on a cooling rack.

When the cake is completely cool, you can start to decorate it. Roll out the marzipan to about 1cm thick and place it over the cake. Brush the marzipan with a little water and then cover with the fondant icing.

Preheat the oven to 120°C/Fan 100°C/Gas ½ and line a baking tray with baking paper. Cut the orange into 2mm slices and pat away any excess moisture with kitchen paper. Put the slices on the baking tray and sprinkle them with a little icing sugar. Put the tray in the oven for 10 minutes, then reduce the temperature to 100°C/Fan 90°C/Gas ¼ and cook for another 20 minutes, until the slices have dried out and started to brown. Leave them to cool, then brush with apricot jam and dust with more icing sugar. For the rosemary sprigs, whisk the egg whites in a bowl. Dip the sprigs into the bowl, then shake off any excess. Dust the sprigs with icing sugar.

Christmas pudding

Some people love a Christmas pudding while others prefer a trifle. For us, Christmas isn't Christmas without a flaming pud so we reckon it's best to keep everyone happy and make both (see page 260 for a trifle). If you like, you can divide this mixture and make two puddings – the extra one will keep perfectly until next year. And just think how organised you'll feel!

Serves 8

200g sultanas or raisins

100g glacé cherries, halved

100g soft prunes, chopped

50g candied peel, finely chopped

zest of 1 orange

zest of 1 lemon

150ml rum, stout or Marsala

100g plain flour

1 tbsp mixed spice

1 tsp baking powder

pinch of salt

125g fresh breadcrumbs

150g suet

1 carrot or medium cooking apple, grated

150g soft dark brown sugar

3 eggs, beaten

To flambé (optional)

100ml brandy, rum or even vodka

Put the sultanas or raisins, glacé cherries, prunes, candied peel and citrus zest into a large bowl. Pour over the rum, stout or Marsala and cover with a tea towel. Leave the fruit to stand at least overnight or longer if you like.

Put the flour, mixed spice and baking powder into a large bowl with a generous pinch of salt and mix thoroughly. Add the breadcrumbs, suet, carrot or apple and the sugar and mix thoroughly again, then stir in the eggs. Add all the dried fruit and mix again with a wooden spoon, inviting everyone in the house to take a turn and make a wish if you like following this tradition.

Put the mixture into 1 x 1.25-litre pudding basin or divide between 2 x 750ml pudding basins. If you are not using lidded bowls, take a large piece of foil and fold a pleat into the centre of it. Place this around the basin and seal with a large elastic band or tie securely with string.

Put an upturned saucer or a folded tea towel into the base of a large saucepan and place the pudding on top. Add enough water to reach half way up the basin, then bring to the boil and cover. Simmer for 3½ hours, then remove from the steamer. Allow the pudding to cool, then store it somewhere cool until Christmas Day.

To reheat the pudding, steam in the same way for at least another 2 hours, longer for a much darker pudding. The longer you steam the pudding, the darker it will get.

When you are ready to serve the pudding, run a palette knife around the edge to loosen it, then turn it out onto a serving plate. If you want to flambé it, heat the alcohol in a small saucepan, then light it. Carefully pour this over the pudding at the table – making sure everyone is well clear of the flames.

Black Forest trifle

Chocolate custard, cake and booze. What's not to like? This is a real showstopper of a trifle and should be greeted with hearty cheers when you bring it to the table. Try it once and it will become a proper tradition.

Serves 8

Chocolate custard

100g dark chocolate, broken into pieces

300ml whole milk

300ml double cream

1 vanilla pod, split

6 egg yolks

100g caster sugar

2 tbsp cocoa powder

1 tbsp cornflour

Trifle

500g chocolate cake or brownies

50g black cherry or Morello cherry jam

100g kirsch or cherry brandy

300g pitted black cherries

200g amaretti biscuits

500ml double cream

chocolate curls, to decorate

First make the custard as this will need to chill before you make up the trifle. Put the chocolate in a heatproof bowl and place the bowl over a pan of simmering water. The base of the bowl shouldn't touch the water. Allow the chocolate to melt, then remove the bowl from the pan and leave the chocolate to cool.

Put the milk and cream into a saucepan with the vanilla pod and bring to just below boiling point. Remove from the heat and leave the milk to infuse and cool slightly.

Put the egg yolks, caster sugar, cocoa powder and cornflour into a bowl. Whisk, preferably with electric beaters, until the mixture is very well aerated, pale and stiff enough that it keeps its shape when you trail the beaters through it.

Remove the vanilla pod from the slightly cooled milk and cream mixture. Pour the milk and cream over the egg mixture, stirring as you go, then fold in the melted chocolate. Mix thoroughly, then rinse out the saucepan and pour the custard back into it. Cook, stirring constantly, until the custard thickens – this can take anything from 10 to 20 minutes, depending on how high you dare have the heat. Don't have the heat too low or the custard will not thicken, but make sure you don't let it boil. Keep stirring.

When the custard has thickened to the point of thick double cream, transfer it to a jug and cover with cling film to stop a skin forming. When cool, transfer the mixture to the fridge – the custard will continue to thicken while it chills.

To make the trifle, cut the brownies or cake into fairly thin slices and spread them with the jam. Sandwich the slices together and arrange them in the bottom of a large trifle bowl. Pour over the kirsch or cherry brandy, then sprinkle over the cherries.

Put a layer of the amaretti biscuits over the cherries, then pour over the custard in a thick, even layer. If you have time, place the bowl in the fridge until almost ready to serve, again covered in cling film. Whisk the double cream in a bowl until it forms soft peaks, then smooth this over the custard. Decorate with chocolate curls.

Hairy Biker tip: For an additional touch of festive decadence, decorate the trifle with chocolate-dipped cherries.

SIDE DISHES, SAUCES AND STOCKS

Buttery mash

Serves 6

1kg floury potatoes,
  such as King Edwards
  or Maris Pipers
75ml single cream or milk
50g butter
sea salt
freshly ground
  white pepper

Peel the potatoes and cut them into chunks. Try to make sure the pieces are roughly the same size, so they cook evenly.

Put the potatoes in a pan of salted water and bring to the boil. Once the water is boiling, turn down the heat and simmer the potatoes for about 20 minutes or until soft. Warm the cream or milk in a separate pan and melt the butter. It really is worth doing this, as it will help keep the mash hot for longer.

When the potatoes are cooked, drain them well and tip them back into the pan. Mash them thoroughly, giving them a really good pummelling. Add the warm cream or milk and the butter and mix well, then season to taste. Serve as soon as possible.

Colcannon

Serves 4

750g potatoes, preferably
  Maris Pipers or
  King Edwards
50g butter
1 onion, finely chopped
100g curly kale,
  roughly shredded
200ml double cream
sea salt and black pepper

Peel the potatoes and cut them into chunks. Try to make sure the pieces are roughly the same size, so they cook evenly.

Put the potatoes in a pan of salted water and bring to the boil. Once the water is boiling, turn down the heat and simmer the potatoes for about 20 minutes or until soft.

Meanwhile, heat 25g of the butter in a large heavy-based frying pan and gently fry the onion for 5 minutes, or until softened, stirring regularly. Add the kale and cook for 2–3 minutes, then set aside.

Drain the potatoes in a large colander, tip them back into the pan and leave them to stand for a couple of minutes. Warm the cream and the rest of the butter in a small pan, then add the mixture to the potatoes and mash them until smooth. Season to taste. Add the softened kale and stir together until lightly combined, then serve immediately.

If you're not quite ready to serve, preheat the oven to 140°C/Fan 120°C/Gas 1 and put a heatproof dish in the oven to heat up. Transfer the colcannon to the warmed dish and cover it with foil. Keep it warm in the oven until needed.

Triple-cooked chips

Serves 4

———

1kg potatoes, preferably
   Maris Pipers

groundnut or sunflower
   oil, for deep-frying

sea salt

Peel the potatoes and cut them into thick batons, about 1.5 x 1.5 x 6cm. Run them under cold water to remove as much starch as possible, then put them in a large pan.

Cover the chips with cold water and slowly bring to the boil. Simmer gently for 20–25 minutes, until the potatoes are tender when tested with the point of a knife and you can see lines and cracks start to develop. Using a slotted spoon, remove the chips very carefully from the pan and drain them on some kitchen paper. Pat them dry.

Half fill a deep-fat fryer or large saucepan with oil and heat to 130°C. Be very careful when deep-frying and never leave the pan unattended. Fry the chips in a couple of batches, until they have developed a crust but not taken on any colour – this will take about 5 minutes. Remove each batch when it's ready and set aside.

Heat the oil to 180°C. Return the chips to the pan, again in a couple of batches, and fry them for 1–2 minutes until very crisp and a deep golden-brown.

Drain the chips on kitchen paper, then sprinkle them with salt and serve immediately. If you prefer, you could cook the chips in beef dripping. You'll need about 1.5kg.

Roast potatoes

Serves 4–6

———

1.5kg potatoes, such
  as Maris Pipers
100g goose fat
2 tbsp semolina
sea salt and black pepper

Peel the potatoes and cut them into large chunks. Put the potatoes in a pan of cold, salted water, bring to the boil and boil for about 5 minutes. Drain well in a colander, then tip the potatoes back into the saucepan and shake them to scuff up the surfaces. This helps to make lovely crispy roasties.

Meanwhile, preheat the oven to 200–220°C/Fan 180–200°C/Gas 6–7 and melt the goose fat in a roasting tin. It must be good and hot. Sprinkle the semolina over the potatoes and carefully tip them into the sizzling goose fat. Season liberally and roast the potatoes until golden. This will take 45–50 minutes, depending on the size of the potatoes. Serve at once.

Potato gratin

Serves 4–6

1.2kg floury potatoes,
   such as Maris Pipers

2 tbsp olive oil, plus extra
   for greasing

1 large onion, finely sliced

3–4 fresh thyme sprigs,
   plus extra to garnish

3 garlic cloves, finely sliced

400ml chicken
   or vegetable stock

sea salt and black pepper

Preheat the oven to 200°C/Fan 180°C/Gas 6. Slice the potatoes to the thickness of a pound coin. Heat the oil in a large frying pan over a medium heat. Add the onion and thyme sprigs and fry, stirring occasionally, for 8–10 minutes, until the onion has softened and browned slightly. Add the garlic and continue to fry for 2–3 minutes, then season to taste.

Grease a 20 x 30cm roasting tin or ovenproof dish with a little oil. Arrange a layer of potato slices to cover the base of the dish. Sprinkle over one-third of the fried onions. Continue layering the potato slices and onion mixture, ending with a layer of potatoes.

Pour over the stock until it just reaches the top layer of potatoes. Season again with black pepper and garnish with a few sprigs of thyme. Place in the oven and cook for about an hour or until the potatoes are cooked through and brown on top.

Rice and peas

Serves 4

1 tbsp vegetable or
   coconut oil

1 onion, finely chopped

1 garlic clove, finely
   chopped

1 thyme sprig

400g long-grain rice

100ml coconut cream

200g frozen gungo peas

sea salt and black pepper

Heat the oil in a large pan, add the onion and cook until soft and translucent. Add the garlic, thyme and rice and stir until the rice looks glossy. Then pour in 700ml of water and the coconut cream along with a generous amount of seasoning.

Bring to the boil, cover the pan and reduce the heat to a low simmer. Cook for about 10 minutes, then stir in the gungo peas. Cook for another 5 minutes, then remove the pan from the heat and set it aside with the lid on for another 10 minutes. Fluff up the rice and then serve.

Braised red cabbage

Serves 4

½ red cabbage
   (about 450g)

25g butter

1 red onion, chopped

1 cinnamon stick

pinch of freshly
   grated nutmeg

1 bay leaf

150ml cider

2 tbsp white wine vinegar

3 tbsp light brown
   muscovado sugar

1 eating apple, cored
   and sliced

sea salt and black pepper

Remove the tough outer layer of the cabbage and cut out the core from the centre. Cut the cabbage in half again and finely slice down the longer side to give long strands.

Heat the butter in a large pan and gently fry the onion until soft, but not coloured. Add the cinnamon, nutmeg and bay leaf followed by the cabbage, cider, vinegar and sugar. Season with salt and pepper. Stir well, bring the liquid to a simmer and cover the pan with a tight-fitting lid. Cook for 40 minutes, stirring occasionally until the liquid has evaporated and the cabbage is tender.

Stir in the apple slices, put the lid back on the pan and cook for another 10 minutes, or until the cabbage is very tender. Remove the cinnamon stick. Great with roast pork (see page 140).

Green coleslaw

Serves 4

100g peas or broad beans

1 small green cabbage, shredded

1 large courgette, grated or cut into matchsticks

1 large fennel bulb, finely sliced into matchsticks

1 bunch of spring onions, finely sliced

2 celery sticks, finely chopped

1 green apple, grated

juice of ½ lime

1 tbsp chopped basil

1 tbsp chopped mint

sea salt and black pepper

Dressing

2 tbsp plain yoghurt

2 tbsp mayonnaise

zest and juice of 1 lemon

1 tbsp chopped mint and basil

pinch of sugar

Bring a pan of water to the boil, add the peas or beans, then bring the water back to the boil. Cook for 2 minutes, then refresh in cold water and drain.

Place the peas or beans in a large bowl with the cabbage, courgette, fennel, spring onions, celery and apple. Add the lime juice and herbs, season with salt and pepper and mix well.

To make the dressing, mix all the ingredients together. Dress the coleslaw just before serving. Lovely with burgers (see page 162).

Mint sauce

Serves 4

—————

3 tbsp finely chopped
    fresh mint leaves,
    plus extra small
    whole mint leaves,
    to serve
2 tsp caster sugar
2 tbsp white wine vinegar
splash extra virgin olive oil

Mix the chopped mint leaves and sugar in a small bowl. Using the back of a spoon crush them for 1–2 minutes to extract the flavour from the mint.

Stir in the white wine vinegar and a dash of olive oil until well combined. Set aside until ready to serve.

Cranberry sauce

Serves 8

—————

250ml cranberries
    (fresh or frozen)
juice and zest of 1 orange
100g caster sugar

Put the cranberries into a pan with orange juice and zest and the sugar and gently heat until the sugar has dissolved. Turn up the heat and simmer until the cranberries have softened and started to burst.

Stir and remove the pan from the heat – you should have a mixture of whole and broken-down cranberries. Allow the sauce to cool and set aside until needed.

Hollandaise sauce

Makes 250ml

50ml white wine vinegar

a few peppercorns

1 bay leaf

1 shallot, finely diced

1 blade of mace

250g unsalted butter, diced

3 egg yolks

pinch of salt

squeeze of lemon juice (optional)

pinch of sugar (optional)

finely chopped tarragon (optional)

Put the white wine vinegar in a small saucepan with 50ml of water, the peppercorns, bay leaf, shallot and mace. Bring to the boil and simmer until the liquid has reduced down to 2 tablespoons.

Place the butter in a medium pan over a low heat and allow it to melt, but make sure it doesn't burn. When the butter has melted, take the pan off the heat.

Put the egg yolks in a heatproof bowl with a pinch of salt. Whisk in the white wine vinegar reduction, then place the bowl over a pan of simmering water. Gradually add the melted butter, just a few drops at a time to start with, whisking constantly, until it starts to thicken. Then keep pouring it in a slightly faster, steady stream until it is all incorporated and you have a thick, glossy sauce.

Taste for seasoning and add a squeeze of lemon juice or a pinch of sugar to balance the flavours. Add the chopped tarragon, if using. Serve warm or if making the sauce for use in the salmon pie with spinach on page 92, cool it by putting the bowl into a larger bowl filled with iced water.

Thai red curry paste

Makes a bowlful

─────

4 small red onions,
    roughly chopped

16 garlic cloves, peeled

12 lemongrass stalks,
    outer leaves removed,
    core roughly chopped

8 long red chillies

8 tbsp chopped fresh
    coriander

8 tsp chilli powder

10cm piece fresh galangal,
    peeled and chopped

4 tsp grated lime zest

4 fresh lime leaves

4 tsp shrimp paste

12 tsp hot paprika

8 tsp ground turmeric

2 tsp cumin seeds

8 tbsp vegetable oil

Put all the ingredients in a food processor and blend them to a smooth paste. This recipe makes more curry paste than you need for the curry on page 90. Spoon the rest into a sterilised jar, seal tightly and store it in the fridge for up to a month. Or put the paste in ice cube trays or a freezer-proof container and freeze it for up to 3 months.

Proper custard

Serves 4–6

250ml whole milk
250ml double cream
1 vanilla pod, split or
   1 tsp vanilla extract
1 coffee bean (optional)
6 egg yolks
50g caster sugar

Put the milk and the cream in a pan with the vanilla pod or extract and the coffee bean, if using – it adds a depth of flavour but doesn't make the custard taste of coffee. Bring the milk and cream almost to the boil, then remove the pan from the heat and set it aside for the flavours to infuse while the mixture cools.

Whisk the egg yolks and sugar together in a bowl until pale and foamy. Reheat the milk and cream, again to just below boiling point. Strain the milk mixture through a sieve into a jug and rinse out the saucepan. Slowly pour the milk mixture over the eggs, whisking constantly as you do so, then pour it all back into the saucepan. Set the pan over a very low heat and stir constantly until the custard has thickened slightly and you can draw a line through it when it coats the back of a spoon.

Strain the custard again and if you aren't using it immediately, put the vanilla pod back into it. Cover the custard with cling film, making sure the cling film comes into contact with the surface to prevent a skin from forming, and leave it to cool. Reheat when ready to serve.

Vegetable stock

Makes 1.5 litres

———

1 tsp olive oil

2 large onions,
    roughly chopped,

3 large carrots, chopped

200g squash or pumpkin,
    unpeeled and diced

4 celery sticks, sliced

2 leeks, sliced

100ml white wine
    or vermouth

large thyme sprig

large parsley sprig

1 bay leaf

a few peppercorns

Heat the olive oil in a large pan. Add all the vegetables and fry them over a high heat, stirring regularly, until they start to brown and caramelise around the edges. This will take at least 10 minutes. Add the white wine or vermouth and boil until it has evaporated away.

Cover the veg with 2 litres of water and add the herbs and peppercorns. Bring to the boil, then turn the heat down to a gentle simmer. Cook the stock, uncovered, for about an hour, stirring every so often.

Check the stock – the colour should have some depth to it. Strain it through a colander or a sieve lined with muslin, kitchen paper or coffee filter paper into a bowl and store it in the fridge for up to a week. Alternatively, pour the stock into freezer-proof containers and freeze.

Fish stock

Makes about 1.5 litres

2kg fish heads and bones from white fish (ask your fishmonger)

1 tbsp salt

2 tbsp olive oil

1 onion, finely chopped

2 leeks, finely sliced

½ fennel bulb, finely chopped

1 celery stick, sliced

2 garlic cloves, sliced

200ml white wine

bouquet garni (2 sprigs each of parsley, tarragon and thyme)

2 bay leaves

a few peppercorns

1 piece of thinly pared lemon zest

Put the fish heads and bones in a bowl, cover them with cold water and add the salt. Leave them to stand for an hour, then drain and wash thoroughly under running water. This process helps to draw out any blood from the fish and gives you a much clearer, fresher-tasting stock.

Heat the olive oil in a large saucepan. Add the onion, leeks, fennel, celery and garlic. Cook the vegetables over a medium heat for several minutes until they have started to soften without taking on any colour.

Add the fish heads and bones and pour over the wine. Bring to the boil, then add 2 litres of water. Bring back to the boil, skim off any mushroom-coloured foam that appears, then turn the heat down to a very slow simmer. Add the herbs, peppercorns and lemon zest and leave to simmer for half an hour, skimming off any foam every so often.

Strain the stock through a colander or sieve, then line the sieve with kitchen paper or muslin and strain the stock again – do not push it through as that will result in a cloudier stock. Transfer the stock to a container and chill it in the fridge. It will keep for 3–4 days in the fridge, or can be frozen for 3 months.

Chicken stock

Makes about 1 litre

at least 1 chicken carcass,
  pulled apart

4 chicken wings (optional)

1 onion, left unpeeled,
  cut into quarters

1 large carrot, cut
  into large chunks

2 celery sticks, roughly
  chopped

1 leek, roughly chopped

1 tsp black peppercorns

3 bay leaves

1 large parsley sprig

1 thyme sprig

a few garlic cloves,
  unpeeled (optional)

You can make a decent chicken stock from one carcass but it's even better with two or three, so freeze your carcasses until you have a few. And if you add a few chicken wings it tastes even better.

Put the chicken bones and the wings, if using, into a pan. It should be just large enough for the carcass or carcasses to be quite a snug fit. Cover with cold water, bring to the boil, then skim off any foam that collects. Add all the remaining ingredients and turn the heat down to a very low simmer. Partially cover the pan with a lid.

Leave the stock to simmer for about 3 hours, then remove the pan from the heat. Line a sieve or colander with muslin and place a bowl underneath the sieve, then ladle the stock through the muslin to strain it. Decant the stock into a container and leave to cool.

The stock can be used immediately, although it is best to skim off most of the fat that will collect on the top. If you don't need the stock immediately, chill it in the fridge. The fat will set on top (and can be used for frying) and will be much easier to remove.

You can keep the stock in the fridge for up to 5 days or you can freeze it.

INDEX

Big thanks to all

We have such a talented team and we love you all. First off, huge thanks to Andrew Hayes-Watkins for making both us and the food look beautiful, and to the wonderful Catherine Phipps our recipe guru. Mima Sinclair and her assistant Jemima O'Lone, our food stylists, have the ability to make a beer mat look appetising, so many thanks to them. And thank you Tamzin Ferdinando for finding all the great pots and pans.

Thanks to Abi Hartshorne for her good taste and good humour – not bad for a fellow northerner – and to the lovely Lucie Stericker, creative director. Amanda Harris, our publisher, thank you for your skill and inspiration and for being such good fun to work with. And to Jinny Johnson, our friend and editor, whose brilliance has given us another beautiful book. Thanks also to publicity manager Virginia Woolstencroft for her expertise and enthusiasm, Elise See Tai for proofreading and Vicki Robinson for the index.

Much love to our management team at James Grant – Eugenie, Rowan, Mary, Natalie, Lizzie and Emma.

And to our friends and colleagues at the BBC who've shared our adventures over the years – thank you all. And a big thanks to every chef and food producer in Great Britain who've fed us and inspired us for most of our lives.

We'd like to dedicate this book to Andrew Hayes-Watkins, our photographer and friend, for his passionate enthusiasm for all that we do. May his trigger finger never wilt!

He's eaten every dish he's ever shot for our books – except those with mushrooms – and much to our disgust he's still skinny. And who knows - maybe one day trifle diving will be an Olympic sport and Andrew will win the gold.

First published in Great Britain in 2018 by Seven Dials
an imprint of The Orion Publishing Group Ltd
Carmelite House, 50 Victoria Embankment, London EC4Y 0DZ
An Hachette UK Company

1 3 5 7 9 10 8 6 4 2

Text copyright © Bytebrook Limited and Sharpletter Limited 2018
Design and layout copyright © Seven Dials 2018

A CIP catalogue record for this book is
available from the British Library.

ISBN 9781409171959
eISBN 9781409171966

Recipe consultant: Catherine Phipps
Photographer: Andrew Hayes-Watkins
Design and art direction: Hart Studio
Editor: Jinny Johnson
Food stylist: Mima Sinclair
Food stylist's assistant: Jemima O'Lone
Prop stylist: Tamzin Ferdinando
Proofreader: Elise See Tai
Indexer: Vicki Robinson

Printed and bound in Germany

www.orionbooks.co.uk

For more delicious recipes plus exclusive competitions and sneak
previews from Orion's cookery writers visit kitchentales.co.uk